the art and craft of
Fabric Decoration

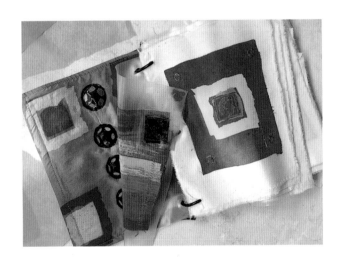

the art and craft of

Fabric Decoration

Juliet Bawden

MITCHELL BEAZLEY

To the staff and students at Camberwell College of Arts

The Art and Craft of Fabric Decoration
Juliet Bawden

First published in Great Britain in 1994
by Mitchell Beazley
an imprint of Reed Consumer Books Limited
Michelin House, 81 Fulham Road
London SW3 6RB
and Auckland, Melbourne, Singapore and Toronto

Editor *Catherine Ward*
Executive Art Editor *Larraine Shamwana*
Production *Sasha Judelson*
Executive Editor *Jndith More*
Art Director *Jacqui Small*

Photography by Peter Marshall
Illustrations by Kevin Hart

This product is suitable for ages 14 years and upwards. We
recommend that children under the age of 14 years are
supervised by an adult.

A CIP catalogue for this book is available
from the British Library.

ISBN: 1-85732-183-9

Typeset in Garamond (Stempel)
and M Gill Sans
Produced by Mandarin Offset
Printed and bound in China

The publishers have made every effort to ensure that all
instructions given in this book are accurate and safe, but
they cannot accept liability for any resulting injury, damage
or loss to either person or property whether direct or conse-
quential and howsoever arising. The author and publishers
will be grateful for any information which will assist them
in keeping future editions up-to-date.

Contents

Foreword

I have always loved textiles; the feel, the drape, the colour and the texture of cloth intrigue and delight me. So it was with a feeling of excitement that I started to write this book.

I was fortunate to have trained in textiles at Camberwell College of Arts when the late Jo Dixon was Head of Textiles. Many well-known designers who later went on to form companies of their own, including English Eccentrics, Pazuki Prints and Anna French, studied with me. Jo Dixon's course was distinctly different from other courses at that time, with a strong emphasis on drawing, innovation and experimentation. These aspects were unlike other colleges, where textile education involved the reproduction of flower patterns in different colourways on a plain background. Jo Dixon is now dead and the degree course that he ran has since closed, however his influence still lives on. Today, art schools are innovative and experimental in their teaching. Most students have the opportunity to experiment with a variety of techniques, often on a single piece of cloth. This has made the job of writing a practical book on fabric decoration a difficult one. However, after examining the work of many new and established designers we have managed to find work that combines a large range of techniques. All the artists featured in *The Art and Craft of Fabric Decoration* are professionals, some of them work solely as textile designers, while others practise in other fields or run their own courses.

The Art and Craft of Fabric Decoration begins with an historical survey of the subject. In a book of this size, this aspect can be only briefly touched on, although additional information is provided within each chapter. The book is then divided into two categories: Painting and Dyeing, and Printing. Within these sections are chapters on the different methods of textile decoration. For example, within the Painting and Dyeing category are chapters on Tie-Dyeing, Batik, Hand Painting, Stencilling, Marbling and Silk Painting; while the Printing section covers Block, Discharge, Transfer and Silkscreen Printing. A step-by-step sequence is featured within each chapter, providing instructions on carrying out the techniques. At the end of the book we include advice on decorating fabric for clothing and interiors. Although it would be impossible to cover every method of textile decoration in a book of this size, I hope the pieces we have selected are inspirational and instrumental in helping you develop your skills.

As the author, my name goes on the cover of this book, however *The Art and Craft of Fabric Decoration* has been produced by a team of people. In particular, I would like to thank the following for their hard work: Catherine Ward, the Editor; Larraine Shamwana, the Executive Art Editor; Peter Marshall, the photographer; Kevin Hart, the illustrator; and Judith More, the Executive Editor.

Juliet Bawden   October 1993

Page 1: This fabric sample book is filled with the artist's printing experiments on silk and rubber. (Ruth Metcalfe)

Page 2: These linear designs were produced using multiple screens. The antiqued finish is created using discharge paste. (Jessica Trotman)

Pages 4/5: A collection of printing and painting equipment.

Right: The artist employed a graphic technique in order to produce this haunting image on silk. First, she covers her drawing with copper foil, which she passes through a press. Next, she translates the foil design onto the surface of a silkscreen, and finally she prints using assorted pigments. (Jane Losty)

Perspectives

Early developments

Throughout history, man has decorated garments and fabrics with patterns, using techniques ranging from weaving and embroidery to dyeing and printing. However, because textiles, unlike paintings and pottery, are fragile and easily damaged by sunlight and general wear-and-tear, few early examples have survived. The earliest printed fabrics date from the 5th and 6th centuries AD (the Coptic period in Egypt), although we have evidence that people were wearing patterned garments up to 2000 years before then. For example, in Egypt wallpaintings surrounding some of the ancient tombs reveal people dressed in patterned clothing and these are believed to date back to 2500BC, while in India it is almost certain that the textile-printing industry was widespread during the earliest years after Christ's death. Some of the oldest surviving fabrics date from the Middle Ages; many of these were discovered inside shrines of the dead. In general, fabrics were left unadorned at that time, although some were dyed in a single shade. Expensive fabrics, on the other hand, such as those found in royal tombs, were more decorative in appearance – some were woven, while others were embellished with embroidery. Printing was a rarity.

The development of textile design during the West's transition from paganism to Christianity was gradual and patchy. Three prominent styles of

Opposite (clockwise from bottom left): A kalamkari *bedspread; a* kalamkari *cushion cover; and a circular tablecloth. All three items are hand-block-printed in India using vegetable dyes. The 19th-century container or* dhokra *is also Indian. Produced in Bengal using the lost-wax process, it is in the shape of a mango. (Joss Graham)*

Above: A selection of contemporary Warner furnishing fabrics, all influenced by early Indian designs. Clockwise from top left: "Flowering Oasis" – the design is based on a late 19th-century Indian hand-block-printed bedcover; "Rajasthan Garden"; "Tree of India"; and "Palmetto". (Warner Fabrics)

decoration prevailed and these overlapped. During the Greco-Roman period fabrics were adorned with classical and pagan motifs, all executed in soft polychrome or single colours. The motifs drew their inspiration from nature and included flowers, birds, vineyards, fruit and trees. Everyday scenes such as hunting were also popular themes, as were mythological events. The second style of textile decoration came to the fore in what is often referred to as the Transitional period, which spans from the 5th to the 6th century, at which time there was a decline both in the quality of materials available and in technical skills. Pagan symbols predominated, although some Christian signs were also present, namely the *ankh* (the traditional Egyptian cross), the *Chi Rho* monogram of Christ and the letters alpha and omega. The third or "Coptic" period took place during the 6th century. Most of the cloth that has survived from this period is decorated with biblical scenes, applied using the resist-printing technique, usually in conjunction with indigo dyeing.

Thought to be the earliest method of decorating cloth, resist printing involves stamping or painting areas of fabric with a resist made from wax, rice-paste or clay. Following the wax application, the cloth is coloured using natural dyes and fixed with a mordant such as metallic oxide or acetate, which makes the dye insoluble when it is washed or exposed to light. As a result, the dye only penetrates to those areas of the cloth that have not been coated with the resisting substance. Coptic cloths were usually decorated in this way and were printed with small geometric shapes before immersion in a woad or indigo dyebath.

From the Middle Ages to the Renaissance
It is believed that block printing originated in China over 2,000 years ago, where it was used as a method for printing onto paper. The technique

Above: This ornate hand-painted Indian wallhanging dates from c.1950. (Joss Graham)

took some time to spread to Europe, although we have evidence that block printing was practised in Germany between the 10th and 14th centuries, where it was undertaken as a craft activity. However, it was not until the Renaissance that block printing started to be carried out as a commercial venture. The earliest surviving block-printed fabric is decorated in the style of gold and silver brocades. Other early motifs illustrate pairs of animals enclosed in a circular shape, although later designs discard the circular border and result in a more overall pattern.

Foreign trade had a dramatic influence on textile decoration and, as fabrics were traded across the world, the art of decorating textiles spread too. In particular, German block-printed cloth was transported along the Rhine to Italy, Sicily and the Orient. By the 14th century, Italy had become an established centre for silk weaving and in later years block printing was carried out in a number of Italian

cities. In the following century, the motif of the pomegranate, which originated in the East, started to appear on Italian velvets and silks.

The 17th and 18th centuries
During the late 16th and early to mid-17th centuries, Italy established a reputation as the main silk-producing country in Europe, with Genoa, Milan and Florence being principal production centres. The damasks and velvets they produced were patterned with graded depths of pile and gold grounds. Popular early designs included small symmetrical motifs which gradually increased in size during the 1660s. In the second half of the 17th century, France succeeded Italy as the principal producer of high-quality patterned silk, the most important manufacturing towns being Lyons and Tours.

The growth of the weaving industry throughout Europe gradually led to a decline in the production of printed textiles which only revived with the influx of Indian hand-painted cottons. The impact on the European upper classes who could afford to buy these wonderful highly coloured fabrics, the like of which had never been seen before, was said to be truly sensational. England first saw Indian hand-painted cottons when she plundered Portuguese trading ships. In 1601, the English East India Company was founded, together with similar companies in France and the Netherlands, to import painted and printed cottons from India. Often referred to as "chintz", the Indian cloth had the added advantage over European cloth that it was colourfast as well as being brightly coloured. Chintzes were employed for both dress and furnishing fabrics. Even the English diarist Samuel Pepys noted in his diary in 1663 that he had brought home for his wife "a chinte... that is painted calico for her line her new study which is very preetie".

With time, the popularity of these new, imported fabrics led to a decline in demand for native wools and silks. As a result, in England weavers petitioned the government in an attempt to ban the wearing of imported calicoes and chintzes. In 1700, an Act was passed in England forbidding "calicoes painted, dyed, printed or stained from being worn or otherwise used within the kingdom". And following pressure from French weavers, a similar law was also passed in France. However, these laws were frequently flouted. As a result, the English Act backfired on the very people it was aiming to help as it provided a stimulus to home printers. To counteract the growth in home printing, the English government placed heavy excise duties on home-printed cloth in the years 1712 and 1714. Finally, in 1720 it was forced to take dramatic steps and passed an Act prohibiting all printing of cloth other than fustian, a coarse fabric with a linen warp and cotton weft. By 1774, the government, realizing that it had failed in its prohibitions, with the demand for printed textiles as strong as ever, was forced to lift the bans and replace them with a series of excise duties that lasted well into the 19th century.

The first successful European attempts to imitate Indian imported textiles occurred simultaneously in England, France and Holland around 1670. The first person to set up a printworks in England was William Sherwin, an engraver by profession, who took out a patent in 1676 for a new method of "printing broad callicoe". However, in 1690 his patent ran out and by 1764 printworks had been introduced throughout the country.

In 1742, the Jesuit missionary Father Coeurdoux carried out an extensive survey of Indian block-printing techniques and conveyed his knowledge to the French. It is believed that his research studies placed France at the forefront of the textile printing industry at that time. Although the earliest French designs were poor reproductions of Indian prints, they later developed into delicate designs

illustrating sprigs, sprays, cabbage roses, ribbons and stripes. Block printing continued well into the 1860s, when it almost died out before being reinstated by the English designer and artist William Morris during the 1870s and 1880s. Morris revived the interest in crafts that had lapsed in the wake of the Industrial Revolution, raised the status of the artist/craftsman and helped the survival of block printing.

Above: A richly coloured odhani *or woman's shawl from Sind, Pakistan, produced with vegetable dyes using traditional tie-dyeing techniques. The ornamental* ganesh *lamp is from India. (Joss Graham)*

Overleaf: A selection of Nigerian textiles. Clockwise from bottom left: indigo-printed cotton; tie-dyed cloth; stitch-resist adire *fabric; tie-dyed cotton; indigo-dyed* adire *cloth, c.1960. (Joss Graham)*

Left: A traditional toile de Jouy *fabric, entitled* "Rustic Scene". *(Warner Fabrics)*

During the 17th century, one-third of all English wools were exported to North America. Consequently, these imports placed great restrictions on the development of the American textile industry. The founding father of cotton printing in the United States was John Hewson, an Englishman, who introduced the first American printworks to Philadelphia in 1773, producing high-quality cloth in the English style. However, it wasn't until Independence in 1776 that North America could start to develop a textile industry of its own. Even with greater freedom, it was difficult and time-consuming to manufacture cotton fibres without specialist equipment and skilled workers. And although cotton, a product of the West Indies, adapted well to the climatic conditions of the Southern states, it wasn't until the invention of the cotton gin in 1793 that cotton could be processed in the United States on a large scale. Invented by Eli Whitney, the cotton gin was designed to remove the seedpods from the cotton fibres; a job that formerly employed the work of up to 50 slaves. Despite this advancement, textile development was severely slowed down by a law forbidding the emigration of skilled workers and machinery from Britain. Although the law was in place until 1842, a British Arkwright apprentice, Samuel Slater, disguised himself as a farm labourer and succeeded in emigrating to America. With the help of Moses Brown, a native Quaker merchant, he installed the first Arkwright mill in Pawtucket, Rhode Island.

Mechanization

The original method of producing printed fabric in Europe involved the use of simple wooden blocks and vegetable dyes. However, after seeing the colourful designs that had been executed in India, European customers began to expect designs of a similar high quality. One of the problems that early British printers encountered was trying to find the right thickener to keep the dye in place on the printing block. It was an Irishman, Francis Nixon, who was to make the greatest contribution to fastness and accuracy in calico printing when he introduced copperplate printing to England during the 1750s. This intaglio method enabled finely drawn images to be printed from flat hand-engraved metal plates. The results resembled engraved book

Right: "Rose and Peony"
is based on a mid-19th-
century French chintz.
(Arthur Sanderson Ltd)

illustrations and worked well as small pictorial compositions and repeat designs. Typical patterns included floral designs and scenes depicting figures, landscapes and classical ruins.

The years between 1760 and 1785 are sometimes referred to as the golden age of English copperplate printing. At the same time, France was achieving equally high standards. In 1770, two German brothers set up a printworks at Jouy-en-Josas, south-west of Paris, France, where they employed copperplate-printing techniques on imported Indian calico. The fabrics were so popular that production expanded rapidly and in 1806 one of the brothers set up his own cotton mill in France, at a time when French government policy restricted imports on Indian cloth.

In 1783, a Scotsman, Thomas Bell, patented the cylinder machine. It was not the first machine of its kind to be invented, but it incorporated a blade which scraped excess colour away from the rollers. The machine was originally invented as a tool to be used in conjunction with hand blocks, although it rapidly became a printing method in its own right. The earliest cylinder machines were powered by water and steam, but with the introduction of electricity the output of printed fabric increased considerably and, with it, foreign exports. When excise duty was finally lifted, the price of printed cloth fell dramatically and, for the first time, cylinder-printed cloth became widely affordable. In competition with Bell's cylinder machine, Ebinger invented a surface printing machine in France in 1800.

In America, manufacturers were constantly battling against these inexpensive European imports. Indeed, printed cloth was in such high demand throughout the United States that in 1824 America was forced to introduce its own cylinder-printing works.

British printers eagerly adopted the cylinder-printing machine as it brought them greater production and increased wealth. To begin with, the cylinders were engraved by hand, but in the early 19th century the "mill-and-die" method of engraving was introduced. This speeded up the process of producing cylinders ready for printing by using steel dies hand-engraved with a motif, which were then rotated under pressure against a softened steel mill which accepted the pattern. The mill was then hardened, making it ready for engraving a roller by rotating it around the surface as many times as possible. Once made, the dies could then be used in different combinations to produce new patterns. It was not until the 1920s and 1930s that the first photographically engraved cylinders were used commercially and these did not become widespread in England until the late 1950s.

At the beginning of the 20th century, the British textile industry was at its zenith. It was exporting 91 percent of the enormous quantity of cloth it was producing. In 1899 the Calico Printers' Association was formed, which consisted of 47 printworks. However, there was a slump in production after the First World War which led to the closure of many printworks. As a result, the people who had once prospered seemed to lose interest, other than in the development of chemical dyes, and Britain fell behind the rest of Europe in its innovations and developments for printing.

One of the most important developments in the textile industry during the 20th century was the introduction of silkscreen printing. Based on stencilling techniques, the main advantage of this method was that it was simpler and less expensive to carry out than engraving a copper cylinder. Almost from the time that silkscreen printing began, people have invented mechanical aids to help speed up the process. The first fully automated flatbed machine came into operation in 1954. It mechanized everything from feeding the fabric through the rollers to gumming, printing and taking the cloth to the drying cabinet. Holland, Switzerland and

Right: A selection of William Morris fabrics. Top right to bottom left: "Acorn" was first printed in 1879; "Rose" dates from 1883; "Compton" is taken from an original Morris wallpaper first produced in 1896; and "Willow Boughs" was designed in 1887. (Arthur Sanderson Ltd)

Austria have all contributed to the mechanization and improvement of screen-printing techniques. In the early 1970s, a flood stroke operation was introduced which in effect doubled the amount of print paste which could be applied with one pull of the squeegee. The latest development in silkscreen printing is the rotary silkscreen machine, introduced in 1954, which is employed in the printing of wide pile carpets and bedspreads.

Design influences

In 1861, William Morris set up his own firm, Morris, Marshall, Faulkner & Co., with the objective of creating a new range of textiles based on the traditions and techniques of the past. The exclusive designs that Morris produced were influenced principally by the arts of medieval England and Wales, as well as by 15th- and 16th-century Italian weaves, and the Indian textiles produced by English printer and dyer Thomas Wardle. Despite the fact that William Morris died in 1896, his influence was the most profound and far-reaching of all the Arts and Crafts designers. His designs, with their elaborate patterns and rich, well-balanced colours, are still viewed as the epitome of good taste in both England and the United States and commercially printed versions are still on sale today (see left).

In 1858, after years of cultural separation from the West, Japan signed a commercial treaty with Britain and the United States, and in 1862 Japanese textiles were exhibited alongside William Morris's designs. The fabrics were an instant success. As interest in the decorative textiles and artefacts of the Far East grew, shops were established that specialized in the import of these goods. One such store was Liberty & Co.. Founded in 1875 by two British merchants, Farmer and Rogers, Liberty & Co. remains the best-known retail establishment today, not least for its own prints (see above right), but also for the way in which it sponsored and encouraged new fresh talent, including Lindsay Butterfield, Walter Crane, C.F.A. Voysey and Christopher Dresser. In 1880, designer Arthur Silver formed his own design studio, the Silver Studio. Responsible for producing a good-value range of textiles for Liberty's right up until 1963, it brought exciting textile designs within the grasp of a much wider public.

The English Arts and Crafts Movement was the pivot on which the reaction to Industrialization and its resulting machine processes hung. In France and Belgium the architects Hector Guimard, Henri van der Velde and Victor Horta developed an organic curving line that came to be recognized as Art Nouveau. In Vienna, Austria, much influenced by the work of Scottish architect Charles Rennie Mackintosh, the craft studio of the Wiener Werkstätte was formed in 1903. Arts and Crafts, Art Nouveau and Wiener Werkstätte designers produced beautiful, hand-crafted prints for fabrics, but inevitably because of the labour costs these were expensive compared to machine equivalents and so were only available to the elite. However, the design motifs had a strong influence on the commercial designers of the time.

While all these changes were taking place in Europe, similar events were also occurring in the United States. In 1844 a school of design for women opened in Philadelphia and this was later followed by additional schools in Boston and New York. The most noted American textile designer of the time was Candace Wheeler, who in 1877 helped to found the New York Decorative Arts Society. Two years later, Candace Wheeler joined forces with Louis Tiffany and together they worked with Samuel Colman and Lockwood de Forest under the name Associated Artists. Based on the same principles as the English Arts and Crafts Movement, their exciting range of furnishing fabrics,

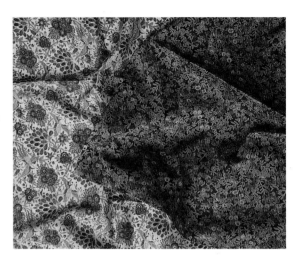

Above: These classic Tana lawn prints are still in production today. (Liberty)

based on simple familiar design sources, were an instant success. During the final decade of the 19th century, arts and crafts societies were formed across the United States.

Throughout history, artists whose main interests lie in other mediums have turned their attention to designing patterns for textiles and the Arts and Crafts Movement was not the only vehicle for this. In France, unlike England, the status of designers was equal to fine artists and as a result many artists designed for textiles, including Sonia Delaunay, Raoul Dufy, Georges Braque, Henri Matisse and even Picasso. Reputedly influenced by traditional Russian patchwork quilts, Sonia Delaunay's textile designs were united by her use of strong colours, blocked shapes and lines. At the beginning of the 20th century, alongside Post-Impressionism, Expressionism and Cubism in the fine arts, the Atelier Martine opened in Paris, France and the Omega Workshops in London, England. Started in 1911 by the French fashion

Right: Dating from the 1920s, this hand-painted chiffon shawl is embellished with gold embroidery.

Opposite: The design for these contemporary hand-painted silk scarves is influenced by abstract art. (Sophie Williams)

designer Paul Poiret following a visit to the Austrian Wiener Werkstätte studio, the Atelier Martine was notable because it employed teenage girls with no formal art training, who were given a free rein to express their ideas. The brightly coloured designs that the Atelier Martine produced were strongly influenced by the naive paintings of the Fauve group of painters.

In 1913, the English artist Roger Fry started the Omega Workshops in London, England. He wrote, "I am intending to start a workshop for decorative and applied art. I find that there are many young artists whose paintings show strong decorative feeling, who will be glad to use their talents on applied art both as a means of livelihood and as an advantage to their work as painters and sculptors." The group, which was made up of many talented artists of the time, including Vanessa Bell, Duncan Grant, Frederick Etchells and Wyndham Lewis, was principally involved in the production of decorated furniture, fabrics and objets d'art. Their designs, which thrived on a mixture of creativity and experimentation, were a reaction against the clutter of the Victorian style and the stylized exoticism of Art Nouveau.

Many people believe that the work of the Omega Workshops, with its Cubist-inspired designs, was the precursor to the Art Deco movement. It was at the 1925 Paris Exhibition that Art Deco made its impact on the world. Ideas flowed from many sources, including Egypt (especially the discovery of Tutankhamun's tomb in 1922). Batiks by the widely travelled American designer Lydia Bush Brown were shown, as were geometric textile designs by the Russian Constructivists.

Textiles were internationally recognized for their valuable export potential. While Italy concentrated its efforts on producing luxurious furnishing fabrics, France was designing traditional and modern fabrics for its couturier industry and Germany was inventing new textile machinery. Scandinavian design was especially influential at this time, especially the natural motifs and clean, uncluttered patterns. In the United States, the Museum of Modern Art in New York launched a public education programme based on good design in 1940, while in the United Kingdom the Society of Industrial Artists and Designers and the Cotton Board were set up in an attempt to revitalize what had formerly been Britain's largest export industry and to educate public taste. Several exhibitions were organized, including "Britain Can Make It" in 1946 and "The Festival of Britain" in 1951, to illustrate the versatility of British design and manufacture following the constraints of war.

From the 1930s to the early 1950s European couture houses made great use of limited edition silkscreen-printed lengths of cloth. Firms such as Horrocks Fashions, Heal's, Ascher and the Edinburgh Weavers become world renowned for their high-quality cloth. The mechanization of silkscreen printing during the 1950s revolutionized the textile industry, as did the development of new printing techniques, such as transfer printing, which was introduced during the early 1960s.

The fabrics of the 1960s reflected the themes and interests of the day – from the first American moon landing to comics. Contemporary art, especially American pop art, including the work of Roy Lichtenstein and Andy Warhol, was translated onto dress fabrics, and tee-shirt designs. In England, designs were based on early Art Nouveau and Art Deco motifs, a style that was adopted by the British fashion emporium Biba. By the late 1960s a strong feeling of nostalgia was in evidence, a style that continued well into the 1970s, when British designer Laura Ashley launched her company using designs based on traditional Victorian patterns.

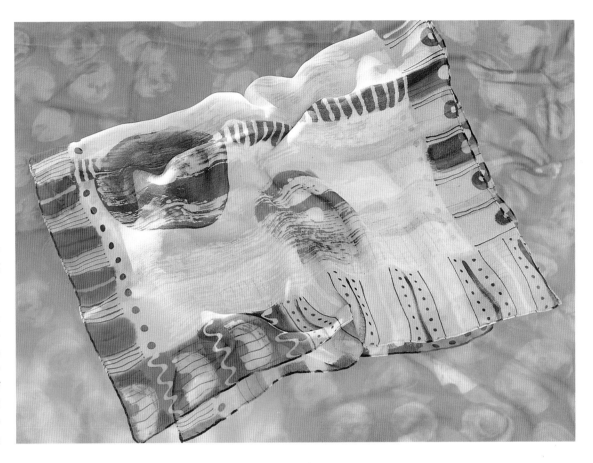

Alongside nostalgia in the 1960s, large, bold, geometric designs were employed. For example, the prints of Marimekko in Finland were admired for their boldness and freedom and were promoted in England by Terence Conran when he opened his first Habitat store in 1964. The late 1970s and early 1980s produced a steady stream of innovative textile designers, including such names as Timney Fowler, Georgina von Etzdorf, and Helen Littman of English Eccentrics. The increased affluence of the 1980s spawned small design groups such as Osborne and Little, Designers Guild, Anna French and Collier Campbell.

Designing for the 21st century
The changes that have taken place in textiles, fabrics and paint technology over the years have naturally had a dramatic effect on textile design. One of the latest developments is CAD (computer-aided draughting), a method that enables the designer to reduce, enlarge and reorganize the components which make up a design on a computer screen, as well as being able to previsualize designs in more than one colourway. Whether these machines will completely take over from hand painting and colouring or just become another tool in the repertoire of the designer has yet to be seen.

BEFORE YOU BEGIN

Equipment and Materials

One of the advantages of fabric decoration is that you can carry out most techniques on the kitchen table with a minimum of expense and equipment. Nearly all the materials that you will need for printing, painting and dyeing can be obtained from a craft store or hardware merchant, although you may have to obtain some of the more specialist chemicals, such as those required for discharge printing, by mail-order (see Directory, p.141).

Before going out and buying a selection of materials and equipment, it is important that you decide which method of textile decoration you are going to carry out since some techniques require specialist colourants. For example, if you are going to discharge print you will need discharge dyes, while transfer printing involves the use of transfer paints. Refer to the step-by-step sequences featured throughout this book for information on the materials required for each project. When you have decided which method of fabric decoration to employ, you must find a fabric that is suited to that technique. For example, while transfer paints work well on synthetic fabrics, they cannot be used on natural fibres, and although cold-water dyes are suitable for colouring natural materials, they are not appropriate for use on man-made fibres. This chapter looks at the range of materials and equipment on the market and examines their uses, properties and applications.

FABRICS

In general, natural fibres are most suited to painting and dyeing since they result in strong colours with more clarity and depth than their man-made alternatives. However, some techniques do require the use of man-made fibres. The following section examines the range of different fabrics on the market and looks at which fibres are most suited to the techniques covered in this book.

Acrylic is a synthetic fibre. It is soft and warm to touch, rather like brushed cotton or wool, but does not stretch as much. Acrylic is most suited to transfer printing.

Cotton is a highly versatile fibre that reacts well to dyes and paints of all kinds. Most cottons have special finishes and for this reason it is best to wash cotton thoroughly before use to remove such finishes and make the fabric more receptive to dyeing.

A visit to a department store will reveal a vast range of different cottons. The following are widely available and are suited to most printing and dyeing processes. Calico is a hardwearing, heavyweight fabric that is suited to stencilling, sponging, printing and painting. Cambric is a lightweight material with a smooth, glossy, crisp appearance. It is ideal for marbling and batik. Cotton lawn is a fine, luxurious, lightweight fabric. It is smooth and soft to touch and is suited to most printing and dyeing processes. Poplin is firm to handle and available in various

Previous page: A one-off silk satin banner, decorated with silkscreen-printing and hand-painting techniques, using acid dyes, discharge dyes and pigment. The artist draws her inspiration from medieval manuscripts and classical music. (Bettina Mitchell)

Right: Painting equipment and materials. 1: Wax pellets for batik; 2: gutta applicator; 3: sponges for hand painting; 4: medium for marbling; 5: stencil brush; 6: large brush for freehand painting; 7: tjanting with two spouts; 8: tjanting with one spout; 9: metallic fabric paints; 10: fabric dyes; 11: silk paints; 12: silk pins.

thicknesses – it can be used for sponging, stencilling, marbling and painting. Muslin is a very sheer, lightweight cotton with an open weave and is ideal for block printing.

Linen comes from the flax plant and is suited to most painting and printing processes. It is generally expensive to purchase, and has a smooth texture with a visible weave or grain. Linen creases badly, although this is often considered part of its charm.

Nylon is a very strong, synthetic fibre that doesn't stretch, shrink or absorb water. It is often mixed or blended with natural fibres to improve their durability. Nylon is widely used for lingerie and hosiery and is suited to transfer printing and dyeing.

Rayon/viscose originates from wood pulp and is one of the earliest man-made fibres. Rayon or viscose is cool to wear and smooth to touch, and is often used as an imitation for silk.

Silk is obtained from the cocoon of the silk moth. It is light and comfortable to wear, drapes well and is naturally crease-resistant. Like cotton, silk should be washed prior to painting or dyeing to remove manufacturers' finishes. Acid dyes are particularly effective when used to colour silk and will produce vibrant results. The following silks are suited to printing and dyeing. *Habutai* or *pongee* is a tightly woven, hardwearing, shiny material. It is inexpensive to purchase, and is widely used for sponging, painting, stencilling, printing, batik, gutta and marbling. Crepe de chine is a lightweight fabric with excellent draping qualities. It can be used for batik, marbling and gutta work. Silk noil is a heavyweight fabric with a rough texture. It is suited to painting, stencilling, printing and marbling. Dupion is a lightweight material with a high sheen. It is suited to sponging, painting and stencilling.

Wool is a natural fibre, obtained from animal hair. It can be spun, woven, felted or knitted. When decorated with acid dyes, it results in bright, vibrant colours.

PAINTS AND DYES

When purchasing fabric paints and dyes, it is important that you select the right type for each technique. Always read the manufacturer's instructions and make sure that you test a sample on a scrap of fabric before you start work. It is often all too easy to become confused when faced with the wide selection of products on the market. This section examines the range of basic paints and dyes and explains how best to use them.

Acid dyes permanently colour protein fibres such as silk and wool. They produce bright, vibrant results and are colourfast.

Cold-water dyes are fixed without heat and are only suited to colouring natural fibres. They are employed widely for batik and tie-dyeing.

Direct dyes are water soluble and are best used on natural fibres. They are easy to prepare and are available in a wide range of colours. The main drawback when working with direct dyes is that they tend to fade after frequent washing. For this reason, it is best to limit their use to furnishing fabrics or garments that do not require frequent washing. Direct dyes are lightfast and are therefore ideal for curtains or soft furnishings that are exposed to light for long periods.

Discharge dyestuffs are designed exclusively for discharge printing and painting (see pp.92-97). They can be applied to both natural and synthetic fibres. Since they bleach away the base colour and replace it with a new colour, they are ideal for decorating black or dark fabrics which cannot be coloured using translucent paints or dyes. Before use, they should be mixed with a reducing agent such as sulphoxylate (brand names include Formusol®, Rongalite® and Redusol®).

Disperse dyes are used in the same way as transfer paints (see pp.102-103). They are not soluble in water, and are ideal for decorating synthetics.

Fabric crayons produce similar results to waxed crayons. Some crayons may be drawn onto tracing paper and then ironed onto the fabric in the same way as a transfer print.

Fabric paints are available in two different varieties: opaque and transparent. The opaque sort is ideal for decorating dark-coloured grounds, while the transparent type can be used only on white or light-coloured backgrounds. Fabric paints come ready-mixed with thickener and are usually fixed by ironing the reverse of the cloth. Most fabric paints are water-based and therefore can be intermixed and diluted or thinned with water. Note: opaque paints actually rest on the surface of the cloth and tend to make it feel stiff, so if you don't want the drape of your textile to be affected by the paint it may be worth experimenting with discharge paints which are actually absorbed into the fabric and produce more natural results.

Fabric pens look like ordinary marker pens, but are specially formulated for use on fabric. They come in a variety of different thicknesses and are ideal for drawing intricate details onto cloth. Some varieties of fabric pen are refillable. Most fabric pens are only suitable for use on light or white backgrounds, but they are ideal for decorating stretchy fabrics, such as tee-shirts, since they are easier to control than paint.

Hot-water dyes are designed exclusively for use in washing machines (refer to the manufacturer's instructions) and give an even result without mess.

Mordant dyes are sometimes known as natural dyes. They have no colour property of their own, but will colour cloth if combined with metallic oxide. Mordant dyes are widely used for block printing and tie-dyeing.

Novelty paints and pens include glitter, plasticized, heat-expanding, pearl, fluorescent and marbling paints. Glitter paints come in a variety of different metallic colours and are available with a special applicator. Plasticized and heat-expanding or puff paints usually come in tubes and are fixed by ironing. Pearlized paints are available in a variety of colours, including gold, bronze, silver and blue.

Pigments must be enclosed in a binder which provides a bond between them and the fibre in order to print with them. They can be used on natural and synthetic fibres and on dark and light backgrounds. They are rub-, light- and colourfast.

Reactive dyes are sometimes known as Procion® dyes or Cibacrons®. They are designed for use on cellulose materials, such as cotton and linen, and reconstituted fibres, such as viscose and rayon. Before use they must be mixed with water, thickener and alkali (washing soda crystals) in order to make the dye bond with the fabric.

Silk paints will produce vibrant yet translucent results when used to decorate white or light-coloured silk. The colours may be thinned with water and can be mixed together. While some brands are fixed by steaming or ironing, others need to be immersed in a fixative solution (refer to the manufacturer's instructions).

Synthetic dyes are produced from finely ground chemicals. They are available in powder, granule or liquid form. No single dye will work on all fibres with the same effectiveness.

Transfer paints are used in the transfer-printing process (see pp.98-103). In general, they are only successful if used on man-made fibres, although it is possible to employ them for decorating natural blends that contain a high percentage of synthetic fibre. Note: when the colours are drawn onto paper they look rather dull in appearance, but they will become more vivid when the design is transferred onto fabric.

Vat dyes are the fastest of all dyestuffs. Because of this, they are ideal for dyeing items that need

frequent washing, such as bedlinen, or for decorating curtains that are displayed in direct sunlight.

OTHER MATERIALS

Fixatives are used to make a printed, painted or dyed piece of cloth light- and wash-fast. Some commercial dyes are available with ready-made fixatives which are added with the dyes. Silk is normally fixed with liquid fix. Fixing can also be done using heat – either by baking, steaming or ironing the reverse of the cloth. (Refer to paint manufacturer's instructions for advice on appropriate fixatives.)

Gutta is a gum-like substance used in silk painting. It is applied to the silk in a linear design controlling the flow of the dyes on the cloth and preventing different colours from bleeding into each other. In its pure form it is known as gutta-percha, while the refined version that is used for silk painting is known as gutta resist. Gutta resist is available with a special applicator as a clear, metallic or black glue. You can colour clear gutta to your own specifications by adding solvent-based glass paint.

Masking tape is invaluable for all printing and painting processes. It is useful for securing fabric to a table during decoration, and for fixing cloth to a frame ready for painting.

Paper is needed for planning your design. Keep plenty of plain paper to hand and buy graph paper for sizing designs.

Photographic emulsion is a light-sensitive varnish. It is used to mask off areas of a screen and is available by mail order from silkscreen companies (see p.141 for suppliers).

Profilm is a gelatine-coated paper which is used to mask off areas of a silkscreen. It can be bought from art and craft stores (see Directory, p.140).

Salt can be used to create special effects on dyed fabric (see p.77). It is also a mild fixative.

Thickener is added to paint or dye to improve its viscosity and prevent it from spreading beyond the

confines of a desired shape. Gum tragacanth is a popular thickener, as are alginate and carragheen moss.

Wax is widely used for resist printing, in particular for batik. Batik wax is available in small pellets from craft stores, although if you are unable to obtain it you can make your own by melting wax candles with beeswax. Note: beeswax should not be used on its own as it is too soft to achieve a good crackle.

Wetting agents are added to the print paste when decorating man-made fibres in order to encourage the fabric to absorb the dye (trade names include Perminal KB®, Silvatol® and Glyzine).

TOOLS AND EQUIPMENT

Blocks are traditionally cut from wood, although it is possible to make your own from a variety of mediums (see pp.90-91 for instructions). One side of the block features a carved pattern which is dipped into ink. The inked block is then stamped onto the cloth to produce a block print.

Brush types and sizes for painting are dictated by the medium or technique you are working in. For example, if you are silk painting you will require a good assortment of high-quality squirrel-hair brushes, while for stencilling you will need to buy short, stubby stencil brushes. Other paint effects employ anything from decorators' brushes and airbrushes to toothbrushes, sponges and combs.

Canvas stretchers are useful for stretching monofilament across a silkscreen. They are expensive to purchase for domestic use, but can be found in colleges and commercial firms.

Cutting mats are self-healing sheets that protect a work surface from scratches. They are useful in obtaining a clean cut when making stencils.

Dyebaths can be made from old saucepans, preserving pans or old enamel baths. Make sure that you select a receptacle that is large enough to agitate the cloth during dyeing. Note: for hot-water dyeing, it is best to use a saucepan since the

equipment and materials 25

Right: Printing materials and equipment.
1: Squeegee; 2: silkscreen frame; 3: fabric paints; 4: adjustable frame; 5: Indian wooden block for printing; 6: fabric paints, ready-mixed with binders.

dyebath has to be placed on a gas ring or hob.

Frames can be bought in various sizes from craft stores. Silkscreen frames can be made from wood or metal – if you buy a frame, make sure that it isn't warped as this will produce uneven results.

Hairdryers may be used to speed drying.

Irons are most commonly used for fixing paints. Fixing times vary according to the paint manufacturer's instructions and the type of fabric used. In general, once the paint is dry iron the reverse of the fabric for five minutes using the hottest temperature the fabric can withstand without burning.

Jam jars can be filled with water and used for rinsing brushes. It is a good idea to keep one for dark colours and one for light colours.

Measuring scales should be used to calculate the percentage of paint/dye and fixative required.

Measuring spoons are essential when measuring chemicals, paints and dyes so that you can work out the exact proportions.

Melting pots are useful for batik work. Specially designed for heating the wax and keeping it at a constant temperature, they also prevent it from solidifying. If you don't have a melting pot, put the wax into a clean food can and heat it in a saucepan of hot water over a low heat.

Palettes are useful for mixing paints, although you could use a small saucer instead.

Pencils are used to draft your design. Always keep a variety of colours to hand. A very soft pencil (such as a 3B) is useful for drawing an outline onto cloth.

Photocopiers are useful for sizing your design before transferring it to fabric. If you are not good at drawing you could enlarge or reduce a picture from a book on a photocopier and then trace it onto fabric. Photocopiers are accessible in schools, colleges, offices and photocopier bureaus.

Pressure cookers may be employed for fixing paints (see p.83 for instructions). Temperatures vary depending on the type of fabric and paint used. Refer to the paint manufacturer's instructions for fixing times.

Print tables should be well protected with a wipe-clean cloth or sheets of newspaper before you begin work.

Rulers are useful for drawing geometric designs. When cutting stencils, make sure that you use a reinforced ruler – this will help prevent accidents since it has a protective metal strip along one edge.

Safety equipment is essential when working with dyestuffs and chemicals. Always wear rubber gloves, a dust mask and an overall or apron and avoid contact with the skin. Work in a well-ventilated area and cover your work surface with plenty of newspaper. Store dyes and chemicals in a clean, dry cupboard, out of reach of children.

Scalpels are the most suitable tools for cutting stencils since their blades can be easily replaced when they become blunt.

Scissors are a must if you frequently work with fabrics. It is a good idea to buy three separate pairs of scissors. One pair should be reserved for cutting paper, since paper will blunt the blades quickly, the second should be reserved for fabrics and the third should be used for silk alone since this snags easily and should be cut with very sharp scissors.

Screens are available from craft stores in various sizes. Silk bolting cloth is the most widely used gauze. The mesh varies from size 8 to 14 (8 being the coarsest and 14 the finest). Terylene is used mainly in industry and is very strong. Nylon can be obtained in the finest mesh size, but tends to become elastic after continual soaking in water. Cotton organdie is the cheapest of all gauzes. However, it is only available as a coarse gauze. Because organdie is fairly weak, it is only suited to short print runs since it stretches and frays after continual use.

Sponges are ideal for making a textured pattern on cloth. If you don't have an old sponge that is suitable, you can create similar effects using old brushes, feathers or even screwed-up rags.

Squeegees are used to force fabric paint from one side of a silkscreen to the other. In general, these should be 2.5cm (1in) shorter than the inside width of the screen.

Steamers are used for fixing paints and dyes. They are expensive to purchase and should only be bought by those that take the craft seriously. If you don't want to invest in one, it is possible to adapt a tea urn or use a pressure cooker instead (refer to p.83 for instructions).

Stencils can be made from clear acetate or oiled manila cardboard. Manila is easier to cut than acetate as it is less slippery. However, the main advantage of acetate is that you can see through the stencil onto the fabric below which makes it easier to align different colours.

Tailor's chalk is useful for drafting an outline onto fabric because it can be brushed away after use. It is available in white, yellow or blue, and can be purchased from haberdashery stores.

Thermometers are needed when working with wax, so that you can keep the wax at a constant temperature of 80°C (170°F).

Tjantings are wooden-handled metal containers with a spout. They are used for drawing with hot batik wax and can be bought from craft stores.

Tjaps are metal stamps used for printing hot batik wax onto fabric. They can be purchased from specialist craft stores (see Directory, p.140, for suppliers).

Trays are used in the marbling process. In general, a marbling tray should be 5cm (2in) deep. When buying a tray for marbling, make sure that you select one that is the same width and length as the piece of fabric you are decorating.

Design Sources

The ideas and inspiration behind the work in this book are as diverse as can be. What inspires textile designers is a very individual matter. In general, they are motivated by a desire to create something new and challenging, but often their inspirations derive from one of the following basic categories – art, history, travel, religion, nature, humour and everyday objects. This chapter looks at some of these design sources and examines how to go about choosing a design for a piece of work.

Before you begin

Before you settle on a design, you will need to decide what you are going to use your fabric for – you may be thinking of making soft furnishings or clothing or perhaps a wallhanging. This decision will influence both your choice of fabric and to some extent your choice of design. For example, while a large repeat pattern works well on curtains, the design may appear lost if the fabric is made up into cushions. And while a small, geometric print may be effective as a tablecloth, the pattern may look insignificant if it is used for drapes.

Colour is a very powerful element in textile decoration – it can make or break a design. It provides atmosphere; it can create warmth or coolness; it can communicate depth or space. Strong colours, like those employed by Dawn Dupree on pp.56-57 can be exhilarating, while cool, pastel shades like those used by Helen Harbord on p.77

create a mood of harmony. While your final choice of colours will depend on your own personal taste, you can also be influenced by the combinations used by others. Some people are naturally good with colour, others are less fortunate. The best way to overcome this difficulty is to try mixing different colours. You can do this by drawing a design onto paper, photocopying it a number of times and then experimenting with different colour combinations until you find one that you are happy with. Always keep notes of which colours look good together. When you go out, look at people's clothes and, if

Opposite: Richly coloured fabrics inspired by ornate metal plates and jewellery. The artist is especially interested in mark-making. She expresses this on cloth by combining embossing techniques with silkscreen printing.
(Karen Smith)

Left: These velvet lengths are influenced by Pre-Raphaelite painting. The artist retains the deep colours and feel for pattern and texture that epitomize the art of this period.
(Isobel Johnson)

Left: A collage on silk, incorporating a wide variety of kitchen utensils.
(Lynn Kirkwood)

you see a combination you like, jot it down on paper when you arrive home. Look through art books and gallery catalogues for ideas and reinterpret the colours you see in your textile decoration.

Nature

Birds, stones, flowers, trees, fish and animals are all excellent sources of inspiration for textile decoration. Nature has long been a popular theme for decorative artists; foliage and flowers in particular have dominated textile design since medieval times when nature was meticulously copied by the artists and craftsmen of the day. Designs can be as complicated as the intertwined foliage of traditional chintz or as straightforward as the stylized daisy that has come to symbolize the work of Mary Quant.

One artist whose influence on textile design has been profound and far-reaching is William Morris. His block-printed fabrics were dominated by stylized floral and animal designs (see p.16) – from waterlilies and tigerlilies to peacocks and daffodils – and they have been a continued source of inspiration for textile designers since his death in 1896.

History and art

Historic reference is another source of design inspiration. Some historical eras are particularly rich in imagery. For example, the designs for many *toile de Jouy* fabrics were inspired by events that took place at the time of their creation – one, entitled "*Le Ballon de Gonesse*", was inspired by the first hot-air balloon ride, while another, known as "*La Liberté*

Americaine", was made to commemorate the American War of Independence.

The Spanish-born painter Mariano Fortuny borrowed heavily from other artistic periods for his textile designs. In 1906, drawing his inspiration from ancient Greece, Fortuny designed scarves and dresses with a modern, timeless feel. While Fortuny's earliest designs were block printed by himself, later he embellished his work with hand painting in metallic gold and silver, which he reproduced from the rich, woven brocades and velvets of the late Middle Ages and Renaissance.

The textile designers Timney Fowler also draw their inspiration from "history, and specifically European art and its rich symbolism. There are

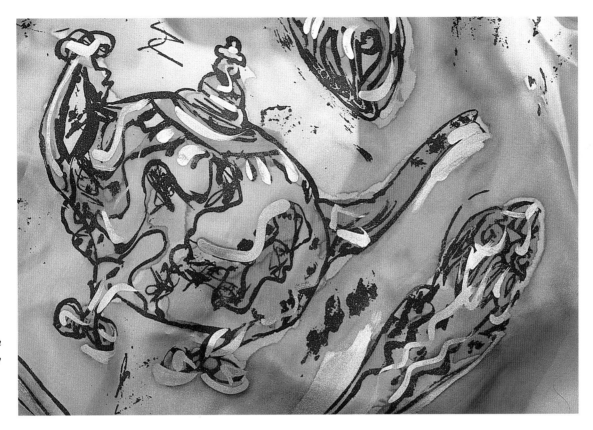

Right: A silkscreen design exemplifies how everyday objects can be elevated into beautiful images. (Jane Losty)

images from Greek, Roman and Florentine objects led by the best-Fascinated selling emperor's heads, twisted columns and classical caryatids vertically ranged" (see p.33).

Museums are a wonderful source of inspiration. My personal favourite is the Victoria and Albert Museum in London, England. It is full of artefacts from all over the world and from different periods, including Indian miniatures, historic costumes, ceramics, musical instruments and furniture. Museums usually have excellent reference libraries containing books on every subject – from costume and fashion to art, natural history and science. Here, too, you can look at historic fabrics from all over the world, including Indonesian woven ikats, French *toiles de*

Jouy, English brocades, Javanese batiks and Persian kilims. The museum you visit does not have to be an applied art museum; it can be dedicated to science or natural history. In most departments you will usually find something which is pleasing to the eye and can be translated into a design for textiles. Start keeping a sketchbook, making sure that it is small enough to carry around with you at all times, so that you can jot down different ideas as you see them.

Travel

Any designer will tell you what an inspiration travel can be. You have the opportunity to see buildings only seen before in photographs; you can look at paintings only viewed before in books; and you can

visit exotic lands that you imagined only in your dreams. Helen Littman, designer for English Eccentrics, writes that "for the designer, travel and the mass media, as a means of opening up the world, are irresistible sources of inspiration. The problem is that obvious cultural piracy is boring; what makes an exciting design is the element of surprise". One of the most inspiring things I have ever seen was a papercut design of a swimming pool by Henri Matisse which was designed to decorate the walls of a restaurant. The papercuts were installed in a room at the Museum of Modern Art in New York and surrounded me on four sides. They were enormous and all-encompassing. I could never have experienced the same from a book.

Zandra Rhodes, the dress and textile designer, has always travelled and uses the imagery from her voyages in her designs. She keeps a sketchbook and makes drawings and doodles during her travels, and collects exciting memorabilia to incorporate into her designs. When travelling, it is a good idea to take photographs of what you see, especially of unusual or finely detailed buildings and objects that might take too long to sketch. Buy postcards to remind you of the places you have visited when you arrive back home. One of the interesting things about travel is that the quality of light varies so much from place to place. For example, if you live in a country with misty, muted colours, it may be an inspiration to visit another country where the sky, trees and general landscape are bright, or where the sun is bleached and faded.

Everyday objects

Design sources do not have to be in the medium in which you are working. For example, the shape of an old piece of china or the colouring of an antique vase or tile may be the inspiration behind a textile design. Jane Losty used teapots to decorate a piece of fabric because she appreciated their imagery and thought it would translate onto cloth (see p.31). At various points in time, certain themes become popular among a cross-section of designers – for example, a few years ago stars were adopted by the fashion and furnishing industry, as well as interior designers and papier mâché artists. While doing research for this book, it became apparent to me that the imagery of the kitchen is very popular today, including everything from balloon whisks to knives and forks (see p.30).

Another way of broadening your imagination is to collect found objects and scraps of material that you find interesting. These might include anything from buttons and memorabilia to postcards and candy wrappers – in fact anything that might trigger

Left (above and below): The designs for these cushions were inspired by the work of The Omega Workshops. (Cressida Bell)

Right: Acanthus leaves and architectural features unite in the sophisticated design for "Masonry". (Timney Fowler)

an idea can be of use. Keep magazine articles that you find stimulating and take newspaper cuttings of special events. Always be aware of what is happening in the outside world – for example, in architecture, music, film, literature and fashion – since anything can influence your work.

Humour

When thinking about visual ideas, remember that wit and humour have a place in textile design. Helen Littman, designer for English Eccentrics, understands the value of the unusual. She explains: "fragmentation of dissimilar images and their subsequent juxtaposition is a design method I often use when working with ideas observed in travels". The designers Timney Fowler also use comic imagery in their work: "wit is introduced by unexpected juxtapositions. Paisley dolphins are teamed with acanthus plasterwork, and animals with a Medici palace facade."

Tongue-in-cheek art reached its heyday during the 1930s and this had a dramatic influence on textile design. One designer was Elsa Schiaparelli, who created witty yet sophisticated garments. One of her most revolutionary ideas was to commission a textile design made from a collage of newspaper cuttings. Everyone thought that she was misguided, but surprisingly the design sold out. For one of her ensembles, she created a design featuring pink snails crawling across the surface of a length of fabric; for another she produced lengths of rayon cloth with coupons printed on top, which she made into a cocktail bag and jacket.

As this chapter illustrates, you can never be too adventurous when planning designs for fabric decoration. Throughout history, unorthodox materials have provided a limitless source of inspiration for the fashion industry and, with a little imagination, you too will find ingredients for successful designs all around you, wherever you are.

PAINTING & DYEING

Tie-dyeing

Often referred to as *plangi*, tie-dyeing is a method of decorating cloth by isolating areas so that they resist the dye. Instead of coating sections of the fabric with a "resist" substance, such as wax, in order to isolate them, areas are bound with thread so that when the fabric is immersed in the dyebath the tightness of the yarn acts as a barrier to the dye and prevents it from penetrating to the tied areas. Other methods of tie-dyeing include folding, sewing or binding small objects such as seeds, pebbles or dried peas into the cloth.

Tie-dyeing is practised in many countries of the world, although the best examples can be found in India, Africa and Japan. The reason why the art of dyeing, and especially tie-dyeing, originated in countries with hot climates is because those are the areas where the best dye-plants can be found. For example, in Africa there is an abundance of wild plants which contain the colouring indigo, the traditional hue used in West African tie-dye. Another reason why dyeing is a native craft in hot regions is because the cloth can be easily laid out to dry in the sun once dyeing is complete.

Traditional methods

Although the methods used to resist the dye may vary in different regions of the world, the actual tie-dyeing principle remains the same worldwide. In Africa, there are two main categories of *adire* (tie-dyed fabric): *adire iko*, where the patterns are made

by tying or stitching, and *adire eco*, where the resist is painted or printed onto the cloth. Patterns of large and small circles are common motifs and these are usually produced by binding found objects such as stones, seeds, beans and marbles into the fabric. Each pattern has its own name. For example, a series of small circles arranged in a spiral pattern is called an *alekete* or *caps*, while *olosupaeleso* (moons and fruits) is made up from five rows of large circles interspersed with small circles. Another traditional method of tie-dyeing involves folding two thicknesses of cloth concertina-fashion into narrow pleats and binding the resulting bundle

Previous page: Two vibrant silk scarves, decorated with free-hand painting. (Kate Blee)

Opposite: Three beautiful examples of traditional Japanese indigo-dyed shibori work. (Niranjali Wickramasinghe)

Above left: The artist produced the background cloth by binding limpet shells with elastic bands and colouring it with brown vat dye. The small handkerchief in the middle was tie-dyed in the same manner, but whole peanuts and natural iron-rust dye were employed instead. The tannic acid in the skins reacts with the iron to produce "iron black". (Vanessa Robertson)

with string. Horizontal stripes can be created in this way by pleating or rolling the fabric widthways, and vertical stripes can be produced by pleating or rolling the fabric lengthways. Once pleated, the fabric is bound at regular intervals to secure the folds. The African word *alabere* refers to fabric that has been stitched to resist the dye. Sewing is carried out using raffia, which has to be stitched very tightly so that it acts as a barrier to the dye. Each *alabere* pattern has its own name. For example, cross-hatching is called "cocoa", while a series of running stitches that make up a pattern is called "three-pences are scattered all around the house".

Translated simply as "to tie", the Sanskrit words *bandhani* and *bandha* refer both to the Indian technique of tie-dyeing and to the tie-dyed cloth that results. Indeed, it is from this word that "bandanna", the English word for a spotted handkerchief, derives. In Western India, *bandhani* shawls are still worn today. These are decorated in the traditional style, with striking white or yellow dots forming stylized floral patterns set against a red background. *Bandhani* is also used to decorate saris. One of the most popular sari designs is the *garchola*, a gridwork made up of tiny yellow dots set against a red background with motifs of lotus flowers, dancing women and elephants. Although difficult to reproduce, motifs and figures are created by binding seeds or stones into the cloth at intervals to form a pattern.

During the 11th and 12th centuries, tie-dyed clothes were adopted by all classes of society in Japan, but tie-dye was also used for other purposes, including draperies at Imperial banquets and flags for ships. Indeed, in 1088 a nobleman from Fujiwara even sailed his ship under a *plangi*-patterned banner. Toward the end of the 12th century, Japanese artists started to develop their own styles of *plangi*, in particular a method known as *kumo-shibori* (gossamer *plangi*) which involved gathering up areas of cloth with waxed thread which was lightly tied during dyeing. Japanese tie-dye is often so intricate in design that it can take as long as a year to tie the knots in one length of cloth and then another year to undo them. Such was the intricacy and rhythm of knot-tying that if a craftsman started a piece of work and had his place filled by another worker, you would be able to identify where the work of one finished and where the work of the other started. In 1683, in an attempt to control extravagance in clothing, the Japanese government outlawed tying.

Modern methods

Tie-dyeing is still carried out along the same lines as traditional techniques. However, the main difference is that different tools have been adopted for isolating the cloth. For example, today bulldog clips, staples and pegs are widely employed, each clamp creating a different pattern. Thus, you can create a chevron pattern with bulldog clips by pleating the fabric concertina-fashion and attaching clips in a zig-zag pattern along the edges of the pleated cloth. After dyeing, the clips are removed and a chevron pattern is revealed. Another method of tie-dyeing is to screw the fabric into a tight ball and bind it with elastic bands. After dyeing, when you untie the fabric, a marbled effect is revealed.

Today, a speedy method of tie-dyeing is to dye the fabric in a microwave. First, tie spoonfuls of lentils into the fabric and bind them securely with yarn. Then make the fabric wet and place it in a china or glass bowl with the liquid dye. Cover the bowl with microwave-suitable plastic film and put the bowl in the microwave. Cook the fabric on a high setting for 4 minutes, keeping an eye on it at all times to make sure that the liquid doesn't boil over. Remove the bowl from the microwave and, wearing rubber gloves, rinse the fabric under running water until the water runs clear, wash in hot, soapy water and leave to dry. Finally, untie the knots and iron flat.

Types of dye

Japanese herbalists discovered a range of natural colours that could be employed for dyeing, most importantly indigo dye, which is the Japanese national colour for workwear. In Africa, a wide variety of wild plants abound, including *Longchocarpus*, *Ficus* and *Jatropha*, all of which contain the blue colouring indigo which is the traditional colour for West African tie-dye and still the most popular hue today.

Natural dyes are still available but they are complicated and time-consuming to use and rely on a great deal of experimentation. For the amateur tie-dye artist, it is probably best to work with proprietary dyes. For example, hot- and cold-water dyes, which are particularly easy to use, are on sale in most department and craft stores (see Directory, p.141). These are available in powder and liquid form in a spectrum of different colours. While cold-water dyes are more time-consuming to use than the hot-water type, they are most suited to tie-dyeing. When working with cold-water dyes, make sure that you leave the fabric immersed in the dye-bath for at least an hour. After dyeing, the colours need to be fixed to make them colourfast. There are various ways for doing this, including steaming and ironing. For best results, refer to the manufacturer's instructions since fixing methods vary depending on the brand of dye used. Procion M dyes are also popular and come in a wide range of vibrant colours. Procion M was developed by ICI during the 1950s and has the advantage over hot-water dyes that it is fast in water. For more information on dyes, refer to Equipment and Materials (see pp.24-27).

Right: The vat dye is capable of producing a wide variety of fascinating blue tones. These indigo-dyed fabrics were tied and stitched in places in order to resist the dye. (Vanessa Robertson)

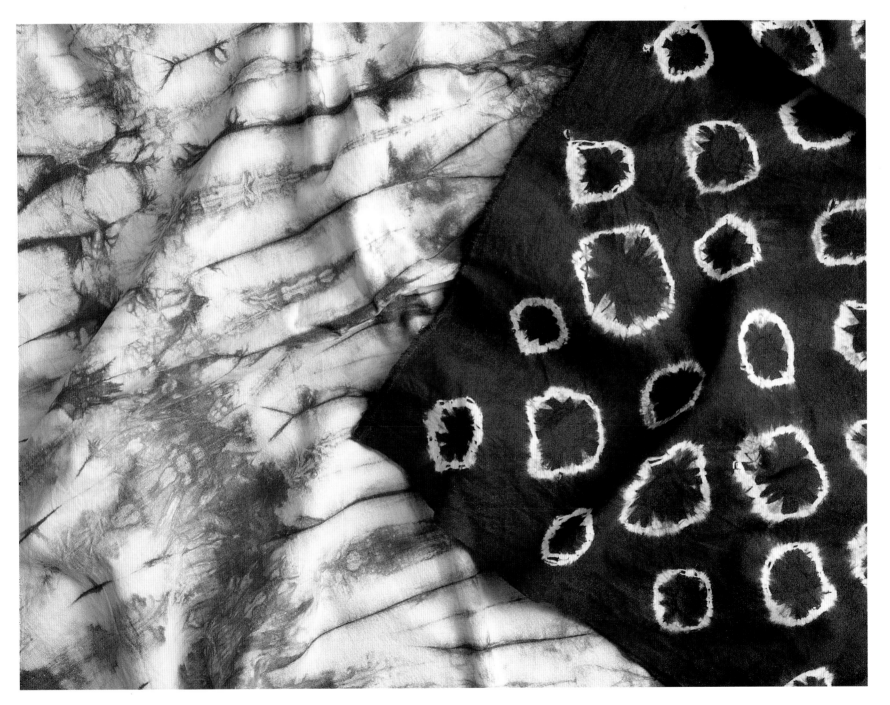

While cotton is the traditional fibre for tie-dyeing in Africa and India, you can use almost any fibre for this process providing that it is receptive to the dye and not too bulky to withstand tying. For best results, select a smooth, fine cloth such as cotton lawn. In general, man-made fibres are not as suitable as natural ones because they don't absorb the dyes as readily.

Always make sure that you wash the cloth prior to dyeing to remove manufacturers' finishes and grease, since these may impair the results. It is

EQUIPMENT AND
MATERIALS

Fabric

Turquoise cold-water dye

Blue cold-water dye

Fixative

Measuring jug

4 tbsp salt　　　　　　**Wooden spoon**

Absorbent kitchen paper　　**Iron**

Rubber gloves

Needle

Buttonhole thread

Dyebath

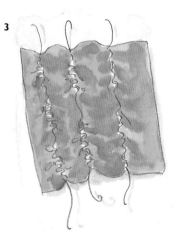

I First mix up the turquoise dyebath, making sure that you follow the manufacturer's instructions. When the dye has completely dissolved, add four level tablespoons of salt and one sachet of fixative (dissolved first in boiling water).

Wearing rubber gloves, immerse the fabric in the dyebath and keep it submerged for at least an hour. When the cloth has absorbed the dye, remove it from the bath and leave to dry.

2 To produce a lozenge design on the cloth, fold the fabric in half to produce two thicknesses and, using a running stitch and buttonhole thread,

stitch a series of curves 10.2cm (4in) in length along the folded edge, making sure that you leave the ends of the thread free between each shape.

3 To produce a repeated lozenge design, repeat step 2 several times. Next, pull up the ends of the threads and gather them into a pouch effect.

4 To make the cloth resist the dye, bind the thread tightly around the neck of each pouch. Next, soak the tied fabric in warm water to encourage it to take on an even colour when placed in the dyebath in stage 5. Gently dab off excess moisture on absorbent kitchen paper.

important that you wash the cloth in the hottest temperature it will withstand (refer to the manufacturer's instructions for advice). Afterward, make sure that you rinse and dry the fabric and iron it flat before you start folding or dyeing.

As the examples featured in this chapter reveal, everyone has their own technique of tie-dyeing. While some people favour stitch-resist techniques, others produce exciting results by binding objects like peanuts into the cloth. As you will see, the results are often diverse, especially if you create your own dye colour. The example shown in this step-by-step sequence has been stitched in order to resist the dye, but you can employ a wide variety of techniques – from tying and binding to knotting, folding, plaiting and hand stitching. For a random effect, clamp areas of the fabric together with paper clips, clothes pegs or bulldog clips. For a spotted design like that shown on p.37, bind small objects such as rice, pebbles or dried peas inside the fabric, then remove them after dyeing is complete.

5 Following the instructions give in step 2, make up a dark-blue dyebath. Next, wearing rubber gloves, immerse the tie-dyed fabric in the liquid and agitate it a number of times with a wooden spoon so that it takes on the dye evenly throughout. Leave the tied fabric submerged in the dye for at least an hour so that it absorbs the dye completely.

6 Finally, rinse the dyed cloth in warm water and leave it to dry. When the cloth is dry, untie the ties and unpick the stitches, then iron flat. Finally, decorate with drawn-thread work.

Right: Segments of this piece of linen cloth were hand-stitched with buttonhole thread in order to resist the dyes.

For a different feel, experiment with other binding materials. These may include any of the following: raffia, elastic bands, pipe cleaners, plastic cord or string.

In order to give her work extra depth and to produce geometric shapes, the artist has drawn out selected threads from the cloth.
(Catriona Baird)

Batik

Like tie-dyeing, batik is a resist method of patterning cloth. The principle of all resist techniques is that a "resist" substance, such as wax or starch paste, is applied to the surface of the cloth to prevent the dye from penetrating to those areas when the fabric is placed in the dyebath. Therefore, when the waxed cloth is removed from the dyebath the areas that have been coated with wax retain their original colour, while the unwaxed areas take on a new hue.

Some theories suggest that batik originated in China between 474BC and 221BC and that the art then spread eastward to Japan. Today, batik is practised in many parts of the world, including India, Africa, South-East Asia and Europe. However, one island, Java, is at the heart of batik design. Indeed, the word "batik" originates from the Javanese verb *ambatik*, which derives from the word *tik* meaning to mark with dots. It is thought that batik was introduced into Indonesia by Indian settlers during the 12th century. Since that time, Javanese batiks have come to be regarded as among the most beautiful and sought-after pieces in the world.

In Indonesia, batik cloth serves a variety of purposes, the most common being for garments. Probably the most widely recognized batik garment is the sarong, which typically consists of a skirt woven in the shape of a tube, worn by both men and women. Although individual styles differ according to the region, the most common design consists of a spear-like motif combined with a geometric design, bordered by a narrow ornamental stripe. Popular colours include red, blue, black and cream, and gold for celebrations.

Traditional techniques

The basic method of producing batik in Java has changed very little since its introduction during the

Left: This abstract piece is entitled "Upsurge". The artist writes: "My recurring theme is about the cutting forces in society which intentionally confuse and fragment, divide and rule ... to enslave the spirit".
(Noel Dyrenforth)

Right: The design for these scarves was inspired by small pods. The artist has employed a limited use of dye and has kept the crackling of the wax to a minimum.
(Kenneth Peat)

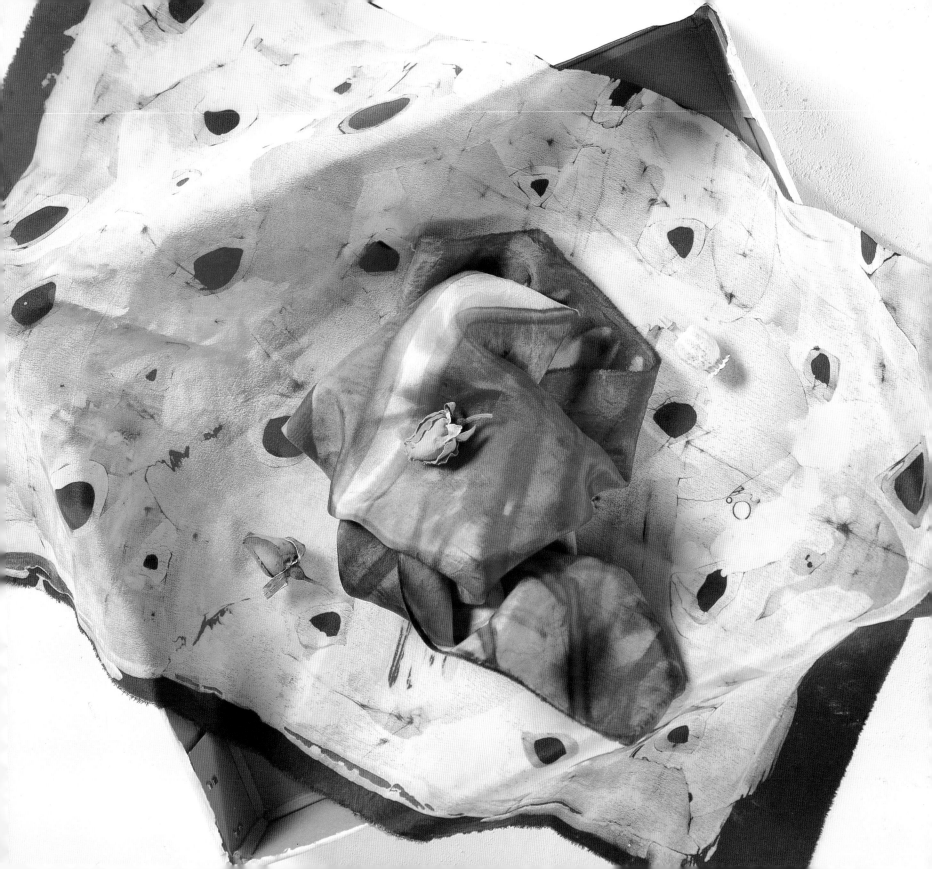

Below (left and right): These traditional wall-hangings are characteristically textured in appearance. You can achieve this effect by crushing or crackling the waxed cloth before applying the colour. This process produces a veined appearance since it encourages the dye to penetrate into the hairline cracks. The artist applies the dye with a paintbrush, rather than dipping the fabric in a dyebath, which gives her work greater definition. (Moira Brennan)

44 painting and dyeing

12th century. Before applying the wax, the fabric has to undergo a series of preparatory stages. First the cloth is hemmed to prevent it from fraying, then it is boiled to remove any grease or dressing. Next, a mordant made from castor oil or ground-nut oil is applied to the surface, followed by a lye made from rice-straw ash. Finally, the fabric is sized using cassava which prevents the wax from spreading uncontrollably across the surface of the cloth. Once these stages are complete, the fabric is pounded with a mallet to make it smooth before stretching it across a frame.

In Java, the job of applying the wax was traditionally a domain of the women, while the men were responsible for dyeing the waxed fabric. Although very skilled batik artists are able to draw the wax design onto the fabric freehand, many batik workers choose to draw an outline first in charcoal. Sometimes a stencil, known as a *pola*, is placed underneath the cloth to act as a template.

It is believed that in the Indonesian archipelago there are as many as 3,000 batik designs, many of which are owned by individual families. Perhaps the oldest Indonesian motif is the *gringsing* or fishscale pattern, which is believed by natives to ward off sickness. Other popular designs include geometric patterns, botanical motifs, crosses, rice stalks and simple flowers. Traditionally, the most highly esteemed motifs were recorded on a lattice of palm leaves and bamboo and then passed down through the generations from mother to daughter. However, today photographs and graph paper are employed instead.

Traditional recipes for batik wax are closely guarded secrets. Originally, Javanese batik workers employed beeswax, which they obtained from Sumatra, Sumbawa and Timor. During the 19th century, ozokerite, a waxy paraffin substance, was imported from Europe and this has been used extensively for batik ever since. Today, a typical wax mixture contains a combination of beeswax and paraffin, together with resins for adhesiveness and animal fats to aid the flow of the wax in the applicator.

The traditional tool for applying the wax in Java is a *tjanting* or *canting* – a copper pot with a number of spouts through which the hot wax is poured onto the fabric. The most prized batiks are worked on both the front and the back. Thus, when the waxing on one side is complete, the fabric is turned over and the reverse side is waxed too. Once the wax application is complete, the waxed fabric is left to set, before immersing it in a cold-water dyebath. Sometimes the batik worker will deliberately crush or "crackle" the wax before dyeing the cloth to create a marbled effect. During the dyeing process, the dye seeps into these cracks in the wax to give the batik its characteristic appearance. After dyeing and drying, part of the wax is scraped away from the cloth before applying subsequent layers of wax and dyeing in contrasting colours. When the waxing and dyeing processes are complete, the layers of wax are removed by immersing the fabric in a cauldron of boiling water in order to melt the wax. Finally, the fabric is polished and glazed by hand using a shell.

Modern techniques

Traditionally, batik was done on cotton and this is still considered to be the most suitable fabric since it is smooth, resilient and absorbent. For best results, select a smooth fabric with a high thread-count, such as cotton lawn. One point that is worth noting if you are working with silk is that it will absorb the wax far more quickly than cotton, while wool, with its naturally high lanolin content, will take some time to absorb the wax. As with all techniques, make sure that you wash the fabric in hot, soapy water and rinse it thoroughly before you commence dyeing to remove any grease or impurities that may impair dye absorption.

Relatively few special tools are required for batik, although it is worth purchasing a *tjanting*. Designed to draw the pattern in wax on the cloth, this instrument is ideal for fine linework. If you do not have access to a *tjanting*, or you need to cover a large area of fabric, you could use a paintbrush instead. In general, a stiff, compact brush will provide better coverage than a soft brush because you can use it to force the wax into the material. For waxing large areas of cloth, a broad brush with natural hair or bristle is recommended. As with all new techniques, it is a good idea to experiment with different applicators on a fabric remnant. For example, you can achieve an interesting, random effect by dripping wax onto the fabric from a small vessel and crushing or crackling the cloth prior to immersing it in the dyebath.

As hand-drawn batik is expensive and time-consuming, a more common method of applying the wax commercially is to use a wax block or a *tjap* or cap. A *tjap* typically consists of a single motif or design made from copper strips soldered onto an open frame. This is inserted into a pan of hot wax and then stamped onto the surface of the cloth rather like a print block. Although not widely available, *tjaps* are stocked by some specialist craft outlets (see Directory, p.141, for suppliers).

One of the most important factors to consider when working with wax is that it solidifies when it cools and is therefore liable to clog up the spout of the *tjanting*. For this reason, it is important that you keep the wax at a constant temperature of 80°C (170°F). An electric *tjanting* is useful for this purpose since it has a built-in thermostat which keeps the wax at a constant temperature so that it flows evenly onto the fabric. The main drawback of using these instruments is that they are heavy and bulky

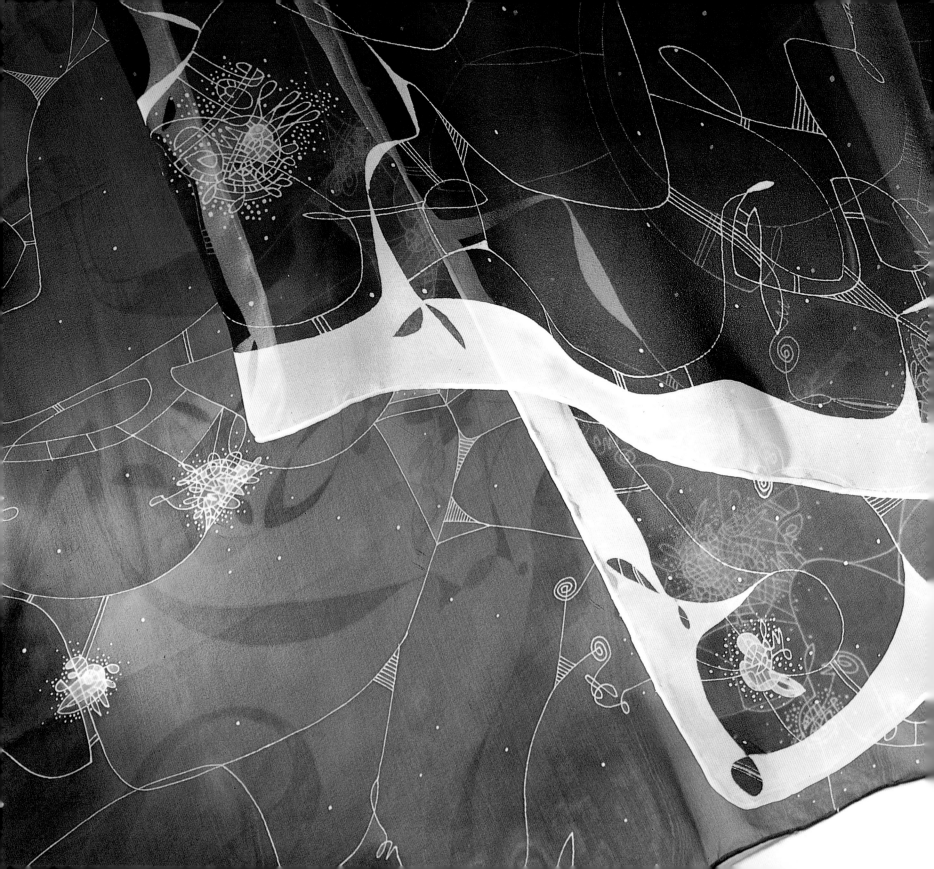

to use. Another useful piece of equipment is an electric melting pot. This is also thermostatically controlled and is designed to prevent the wax from overheating in the pan. If you don't have access to a melting pot, you could use a bain-marie and a thermometer instead. As with all hot liquids, wax can be dangerous if it is spilt on the skin. Today, a popular substitute for wax is gutta, a resisting liquid that works on the same principles as wax but doesn't need heating prior to application. Applied using a special disposable tube, gutta flows slowly onto the fabric without clogging, thus allowing the user more freedom of design (see pp.80-81).

The original colours used for dyeing batik in Java are indigo blue and soga brown. Unique to Indonesia, soga brown originates from tree bark which is chopped and soaked in a mordant. For the modern batik artist, there are many different varieties of paint and dye to choose from, the most appropriate being cold-water and reactive dyes. These are available in a spectrum of colours and are not prone to bleed when the dyed fabric is boiled to remove the

wax (for more information on dyes, see pp.22-27). When working with cold-water dyes, make sure that you keep the dye and the fixative in separate containers until you are ready to use them. Add the dye to the dyebath at the last possible moment since the fixative will only remain stable for about two hours once mixed with the dye.

If you are dyeing fabric in more than one colour, first paint over the background areas, say white, with wax to block them so that they resist the dye. Then immerse the fabric in the lightest dyebath, say yellow. When the cloth is dyed, leave it to dry and then apply wax to the areas that you want to remain yellow. You have now preserved the ground colour and the yellow details. Next, immerse the fabric in a darker shade, say blue, and continue waxing and dyeing in the same manner. Note that the final dyebath is always the deepest colour.

After dyeing, the wax needs to be removed from the fabric. This can be done in a number of ways. Surface wax can be scraped away using a palette knife, after which the fabric can be boiled in hot water to remove any ingrained wax. Never pour waxy water down the sink because it is liable to block the drains. First leave the water to cool at room temperature before scraping off the hard wax from the surface and disposing of the water. Do not reuse wax after application; its adhesive qualities will have been exhausted during the boiling process. Another popular method of wax removal is to iron the fabric between two sheets of paper and, although not environmentally friendly, some people remove the wax by soaking the fabric in petrol or white spirit. When working with white spirit or petrol always exercise extreme caution. Work in a well-ventilated area, away from naked flames. A good commercial method for removing wax is to dry-clean several pieces of batik cloth together in a dry-cleaning machine.

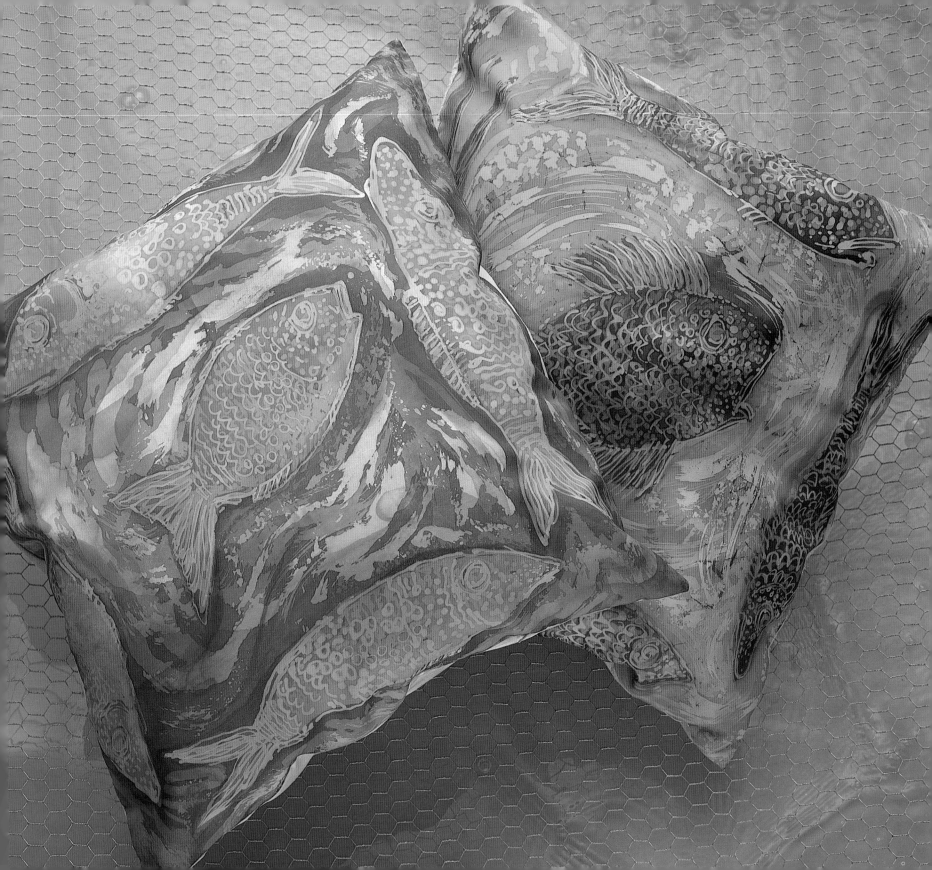

how to make a batik

The application of the melted wax may be done in a variety of ways. As with all new techniques, experiment with different implements on a fabric remnant before starting a project. We have used a paintbrush to cover large areas of cloth and a *tjanting* for applying small details. However, you can create a wide range of exciting effects using anything from a sponge to a rag. If you use a brush, make sure that you dip it in the hot wax at regular intervals to prevent the wax from cooling and clogging the bristles.

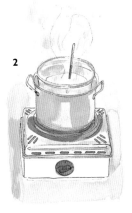

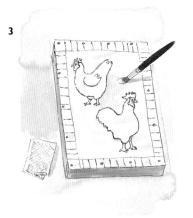

EQUIPMENT AND MATERIALS

Thick marker pen

Scrap paper

Masking tape

Cotton fabric

Batik stretcher

Three-pronged silk pins or drawing pins

Tjantings in various sizes

Paintbrush

Thermometer

Cold-water or reactive dyes

Batik wax

Charcoal pencil

Shallow dyebath

Rubber gloves

Tissues

Electric ring

Double boiler

Iron

1 Using a thick marker pen, draw your design to the exact proportions on rough paper, then secure your drawing to a flat surface or table with masking tape.

Next, wash out any finish from your chosen fabric, allow it to dry then iron it flat. Tape the fabric over your paper design and, using a charcoal pencil, carefully trace the design onto the cloth. Stretch the fabric over a batik frame and secure it with drawing pins or silk pins.

2 Place the wax mixture in a double boiler and heat to a constant temperature of 80°C (170°F) over an electric ring. Top up the lower pan with water at regular intervals.

3 Using a paintbrush, apply a generous coat of wax to the white background area of the design, making sure that you leave the chicken pattern and borders unwaxed. Hold a piece of tissue in your spare hand to catch any drips from the paintbrush. Leave the waxed fabric to cool.

4 Next, start making up the yellow dyebath. If you plan to use more than one colour, make sure that you start with the lightest colour and then progress to the darker colours. For example, go from yellow to red to green to indigo. Remove the fabric from the frame and, wearing rubber gloves, immerse it in the dyebath for at least 30 minutes (refer to the manufacturer's instructions).

Right: You can achieve interesting textured effects by crushing or crackling the waxed cloth before immersing it in the final dyebath.

In this instance, the crackling process becomes an inherent part of the design: it gives the chickens a distinctive mottled appearance akin to feathers.

In order to produce this effect, you will need to use a brittle wax. A mixture of three parts beeswax to seven parts paraffin wax is ideal. (Angela Newport)

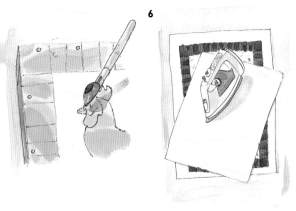

6

5 Remove the cloth from the dyebath and leave to dry before restretching it over the frame. Next, using a fine-nibbed *tjanting*, apply wax over the areas that you want to remain yellow – for example, the feet and the beaks. Leave the wax to dry, then immerse the cloth in the red dyebath. Continue waxing and dyeing in this manner until you reach the final dyeing stage. When you have given the fabric its last coat of wax, screw it into a tight ball in order to crackle the wax, then submerge it in the indigo dyebath.

6 Once you have achieved your desired effect, remove the wax by dipping the cloth in boiling water and ironing it between sheets of paper.

Hand Painting

One of the most versatile methods of decorating cloth, hand painting is becoming increasingly easy to carry out as a wider range of fabric paints, dyes and pens become available to the public. Hand painting fabric has the advantage that you can combine a variety of different techniques and paint mediums on one piece of cloth with exciting results. For example, Rosalind Kennedy silkscreens her work and then embellishes it with metallic pigments to give the silk a unique, painterly appearance (see pp.60-61), while Dawn Dupree produces large-scale, one-off wallhangings by combining discharge printing techniques with hand-painted pigments and dyes (see p.58).

Before you begin

As with all products, it is worth experimenting on a fabric remnant beforehand so that you can get the feel of the paint and the applicator that you are using. Fabric is more pliable than paper, so before you start work it is a good idea to stretch your fabric across a frame to create a taut surface on which to paint. A canvas stretcher is ideal for this purpose, although if you are only decorating a small piece of cloth you could use an embroidery hoop or tapestry frame instead. If you don't have anything suitable, simply tape your fabric to a table using masking tape. This will prevent the fabric from moving around and stop it from wrinkling as you paint it. If you do decide to work at a table,

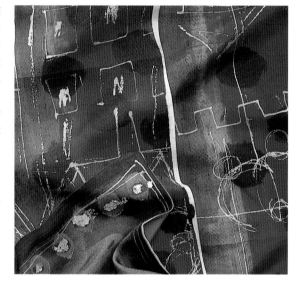

make sure that you place a backing cloth under your material to absorb excess colour and prevent the reverse from smudging – this is especially important if you are working with sheer fabrics. If you are using a frame, it is best to secure the fabric with masking tape as this is easy to remove after painting and will not leave any marks. While you could use drawing pins or tacks instead, these are often difficult to remove from a wooden frame and are liable to tear the fabric. Note: if you do use tacks, make sure that you buy the stainless steel variety as these are not prone to rusting.

Left: The artist silkscreen-printed this cloth before applying gold pigment in a linear design using a fine artist's brush.
(Antonia Phillips)

Right: These silk scarves were hand-painted using acid dyes.
(Maggie Levien)

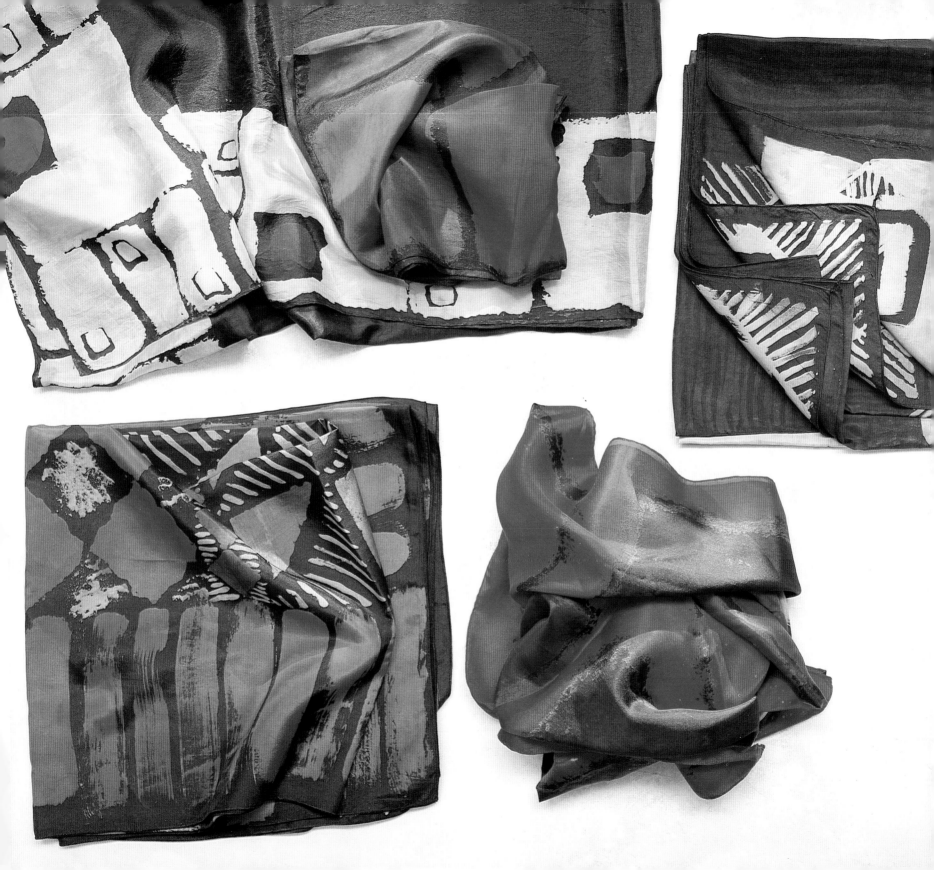

Choosing a fabric

If you are decorating fabric for the home or to make up into clothing, your choice of cloth is usually determined by the article that you are making. For example, loose covers require a hardwearing fabric, while curtains require one that drapes well. Clothing fabric, on the other hand, should be comfortable to wear and should be suitable for washing and dry-cleaning. When you have selected your fabric, bear in mind that its weight and texture will have a bearing on the painted results. For example, a smooth, textured weave will absorb the paint freely, while a coarse, loosely woven fabric will not absorb the paint to the same extent. When decorating heavy-duty textiles, such as furnishing fabrics, it is best to use a robust paint, applied using bold strokes. The weight and colour of the fabric may also affect the resulting colour of the paint. For example, while red paint will look strong and bright on heavyweight cotton, it will appear much paler in comparison when used to decorate sheer fabrics.

The fibre that you select will also have a bearing on your choice of paint. Natural fibres are probably the most suitable for painted decoration since, unlike man-made fibres, they absorb the paint readily and so results have greater clarity and depth. If you choose to work with cotton, make sure that you wash the cloth beforehand to pre-shrink it. Laundering will also remove manufacturers' finishes (which impair the flow of the dye) and improve the cloth's efficiency to absorb the paint. Wool is highly absorbent and, as a result, you will probably need to use as much as twice the amount of paint that you would normally use for other fabrics. Although man-made fibres are an inexpensive alternative, they rarely produce such good results as their natural equivalents, except when working with transfer paints, because they don't absorb the dye as readily.

Drawing your design

While some textile designers choose to draw their design freehand onto cloth, others prefer to plan their design on paper beforehand and then transfer it to cloth because this method gives them more control over the design. If you are not very good at drawing, you can select a design from a book or magazine, reduce or enlarge it on a colour or black-and-white photocopier and then transfer it to cloth. There are a variety of different ways of doing this. For example, if you are working on a sheer fabric, such as muslin, silk georgette or chiffon, you can trace over the design and onto the fabric using tailor's chalk or a soft pencil (3B). If your fabric is too thick and you are unable to see through it, place it on a lightbox with the paper. The bright light improves the transparency of the cloth and makes it easier to see through the fabric and onto the paper template. Another method of transferring the design to fabric is to use dressmaker's carbon paper.

Selecting a brush

The type of paint applicator you choose will also affect the finished product. Depending on the size of your brush and the thickness or texture of the cloth you are decorating, your work may be bold or delicate, subtle or bright. You can vary the finish by using a whole range of different brushes. Household and decorator's brushes will give a coarse, random design, while Chinese brushes will produce a smooth, delicate finish. Use your imagination when selecting a brush. You can create diverse and unique effects with anything from toothbrushes and stencilling brushes to combs, rollers and airbrushes. However, not all textile paints need to be applied with a brush – some are available in ready-to-use plastic applicators, while others are produced in pen form with both fine and thick "nibs".

Opposite: Fashion accessories in silk and cotton, boldly decorated using hand-painting and silkscreen-printing techniques. The vividly coloured images are abstractions of geometric shapes.
(Anne-Marie Cadman)

Above: "Let's Hear it for the Birds" was created using a variety of techniques. First, the artist hand painted the background, then she overprinted the images using eight different screens.
(Audrey Kelly)

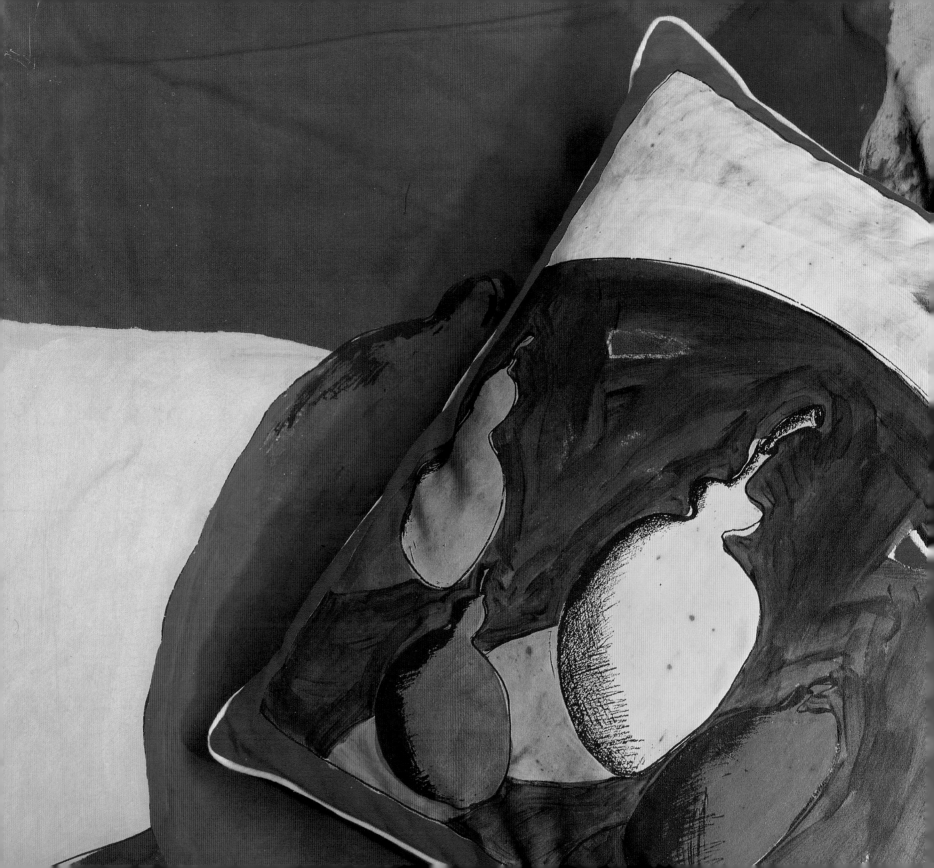

Previous page: Two dyed, painted and printed cushions are set against a background of one-off wallhangings.
(Dawn Dupree)

Right: A collection of wool scarves, hand painted in vivid colours using acid dyes.
(Trisha Needham)

Opposite: The artist combined hand painting with screen printing to produce this one-off wall-hanging. His inspirations are diverse. They include art, design, world events and ecology.
(Pete Shaw)

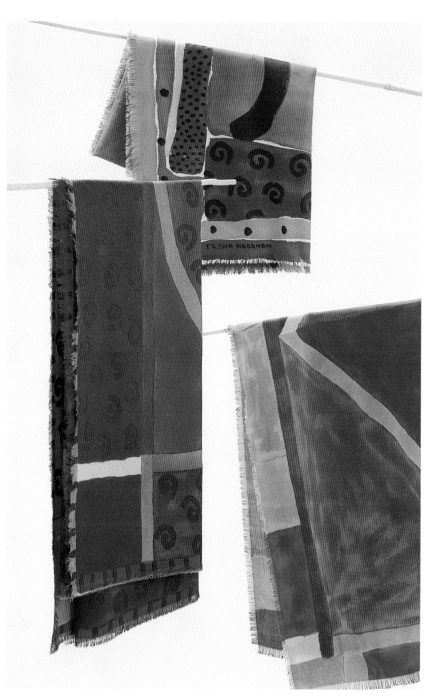

Sponging is a popular method of applying texture to fabric and is often carried out in conjunction with other paint finishes. The fabric shown on p.69 was sponged first and then stencils were applied by hand afterward. For more information on sponging, refer to the step-by-step sequence on pp.62-63.

Another popular method of creating textured backgrounds on cloth is to use a diffuser. Diffusers are designed to create a fine, misty haze on the surface of material and are quick and easy to use. When working with a diffuser, make sure that you dilute the paint to a watery consistency before use, otherwise it is liable to block the outlet. If you don't have access to a diffuser, you could employ a household plant mister instead or simply dip an old toothbrush into paint and flick it across the surface of the cloth.

Choosing the paint

Fabric paints are available in two basic sorts – those that are absorbed into the fabric and those that rest on the surface of the cloth. While both varieties are suitable for painting light-coloured backgrounds, if you intend to work on a dark ground you will need to select the sort that rests on the surface of the cloth. This is most important in order to preserve a clear outline and to prevent the background colour from showing through. The main drawback of working with opaque fabric paints is that they do tend to stiffen the fabric, which affects the drape of the cloth. So, although they are acceptable for furnishing fabrics, blinds and cushion covers, they don't work as well on garments.

The paint manufacturers should state on the packaging whether the product is suitable for synthetic or natural fibres or both. They should also explain whether their particular brand is suitable for decorating dark colours, or should be used only on pale backgrounds. It isn't necessary to buy a vast range of colours for fabric painting. A small variety of primary colours, plus black and white, will enable you to mix a large spectrum of colours. When mixing pastel shades, always add the colour to the white a drop at a time, not the other way around. If you do decide to mix different colours, note that it may be difficult to obtain exactly the same shade a second time so make sure that you make up enough colour to complete the job.

When fabric paints were first developed for domestic use, they came mixed with binders in jars and had to be applied using a paintbrush. However, in recent years a whole range of developments do heat-expanding paints, also known as "puff paints" or "slick sticks". Note that these are not suitable for decorating clothing that needs frequent laundering because the paint is inclined to peel off after regular washing. Heat-expanding paints are simple to use. Simply draw your design on the surface of the cloth, then turn it over and iron the reverse for a couple of minutes, or until the paint expands. Beading paints are an interesting alternative to fabric paints and can be used to great effect on anything – from teatowels and garments to borders and bedlinen.

mark as soon as they come into contact with the fabric, while others can be removed if washed with soap and water. You can also produce interesting effects with a wax fabric crayon. By placing a textured item, such as a coin, a leaf or a piece of tree-bark, underneath the cloth you can create an interesting frottage result by rubbing over the textured surface with a crayon. Another exciting method of using colour is to create a monoprint. To do this, simply apply the fabric paint to a sheet of glass or Formica with a squeegee and scratch out a design on the glass with a cocktail stick, needle or

have taken place which have lead to a more sophisticated range of products. While you can still buy fabric paints in pots, today they are also available in tubes, applicators, crayons, pens and sprays. The range of paints is endless. You can buy glitter paints, heat-expanding paints, aqueous inks, fluorescent paints, metallic paints, marker pens and even transfer paints. Simply choose a fabric and select a paint medium to suit the quality of fabric you are working with. For example, glitter paints work well on tee-shirts and dark-coloured backgrounds, as

You can create a profusion of different designs using marker pens. Drawing is probably the easiest method of decorating cloth and can be used to produce a whole variety of different designs – from paisley patterns to checks, plaids and stripes. Marker pens are similar to felt-tipped pens and are applied in the same way. They are available in a wide assortment of colours and with different-sized nibs. For example, some have fine points for outlining, while others have wide nibs for drawing broad lines and filling. Some brands form a permanent

comb. Then press the fabric carefully onto the painted surface to transfer the design.

Fixing methods for fabric paints usually involve ironing the reverse of the fabric for about five minutes, using the hottest setting the fabric can withstand without burning. Note that when fixing crayons, you should place a piece of cloth between the fabric and the iron to prevent the wax from sticking to the hot iron. If you are in doubt about which fixing method to use, refer to the paint manufacturer's instructions.

hand painting 59

how to use metallic paint

The silk banners shown opposite were decorated by hand using metallic pigments. These are designed to rest on the surface of the cloth, rather like gold leaf, instead of being absorbed into the fabric like acid or silk paints.

The main drawback of working with metallic pigments is that they need to be dried in a special infra-red cabinet (they don't dry naturally at room temperature). For this reason, metallic pigments are not suited to domestic use.

EQUIPMENT AND MATERIALS

Scrap paper

Coloured pens

Soft pencil or tailor's chalk

Old sheet

Backing cloth

Silk fabric

Dressmaker's pins

Masking tape   **Paintbrushes**

Metallic paste   **Iron**

Binder   **Cold-water or hot-water dyes (optional)**

Catalyst

Bowl

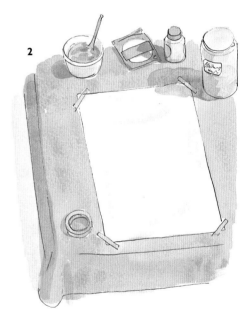

I First draw your design on rough paper, using the actual colours that you intend to use for your final design. If you don't have the exact colours, indicate where they should go using a lead pencil.

If you are unable to buy silk in your preferred shade, dye a piece of white silk using hot- or cold-water dyes. Leave the cloth to dry and fix the colour by ironing the reverse of the cloth.

When fixing dyes or paints, always use the hottest setting that the fabric can withstand without burning.

2 Cover a work surface with an old sheet or a piece of lining fabric to protect it, then place a backing cloth over the top and secure it with masking tape.

Following the manufacturer's instructions for quantities, combine the binder with the catalyst.

In order to produce a similar effect to metallic pigments, we suggest that you use metallic paste, combined with a binder and a catalyst. Metallic paste can be dried conventionally and has the advantage over normal fabric paints that it doesn't require fixing. If you are unable to obtain metallic paste, binder or catalyst, you could use metallic pens instead. Metallic pens are simple to use and are obtainable from craft stores (see Directory, p.141 for suppliers).

Right: Classical music, calligraphy and all things baroque provide the inspiration and themes for these silk banners.

First, the artist dyes the cloth in strong, eye-catching colours, then she silkscreen prints musical scripts across the surface and, finally, she embellishes the material by hand using metallic pigments.

If you do not want to dye the cloth by hand, you could achieve a similar effect by decorating a piece of ready-dyed cloth. (Rosalind Kennedy)

3

4

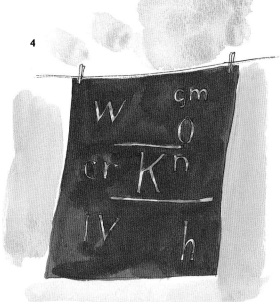

Once the catalyst is added, the mixture must be used within 24 hours. Next, combine the binder with the metallic paste in a bowl.

3 Pin the dyed silk securely to the backing fabric and, using a soft pencil or a piece of tailor's chalk, draw your design on the silk to the exact dimensions.

Next, dip a fine paintbrush into the metallic paste mixture and carefully trace over the pencil guidelines. Vary the thickness of your paintbrush according to how heavy or fine a line you want to produce.

4 Once you are satisfied with your painted design, unpin the silk, carefully lift it off the work surface and hang it in a warm room to dry. It is important that you leave the metallic paste to dry for at least 48 hours before attempting to wash the cloth.

how to sponge

Sponging is a simple and effective method of adding texture to cloth, and produces excellent results when used as a background for other decorative finishes such as stencilling or block printing. However, this technique does not have to be carried out with a sponge – you can create similar effects by printing with screwed-up pieces of cloth or kitchen paper.

To achieve a successful result, make sure that you dab off excess paint from the sponge onto

EQUIPMENT AND MATERIALS

Fabric

Iron

Print table

Masking tape

Fabric paints

Saucer

Sponge

Absorbent kitchen paper

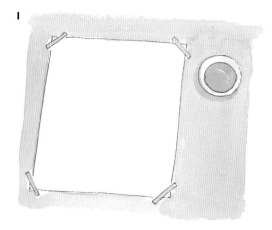

I As with all painting and dyeing projects, it is important that before you start sponging you wash your selected cloth in hot, soapy water to remove grease or manufacturers' finishes. Next, rinse the cloth under clear, running water and leave to dry before ironing flat. Place the prepared cloth on a print table and secure the corners with masking tape.

Pour a little fabric paint into a clean saucer and dilute it with enough water to produce a pale colour and a "single cream" consistency.

2 Dip a clean, dry sponge into the saucer of paint, then dab off any excess paint onto absorbent kitchen paper. Gently dab the sponge in random patches over the prepared cloth, making sure that you leave gaps between the individual marks. As the colour on the cloth starts to lighten and the sponge begins to dry out, dip it into the paint again, dab off excess colour on absorbent kitchen paper and continue sponging in the same manner.

Once you are satisfied with the first colour application, leave the fabric to dry flat before applying additional colour in the same way. While the fabric is drying, rinse the sponge in warm water and leave it to dry. It is important

absorbent kitchen paper before you apply the sponge to the fabric. This will prevent the design from looking smudged and watery.

If you choose to sponge in more than one colour, it is best to start with the lightest shade first and then progress to the darker colours. A simple method of doing this is to thin the first shade of fabric paint with water and and then add a darker shade of paint, a little at a time, until the desired hue is arrived at.

Right: Sponging may be applied as a technique by itself, or in conjunction with other decorative finishes. The artist sponged these cotton cushions in two complementary shades and then applied stencils by hand afterward.

The cotton button makes an attractive alternative to a zip fastener. The artist covered this one with a remnant of blue sponged cloth. (Ruth Pringle)

that the sponge is completely dry when it is dipped into the paint, since a wet sponge will dilute the paint further and result in a smeary image on the cloth.

3 To create a deeper shade of fabric paint, pour a couple of drops of undiluted paint into the diluted mixture already in the saucer and mix the colours together until the desired colour is arrived at. The second colour should be the consistency of "double cream".

Next, dip the clean, dry sponge into the paint, dab off any excess moisture onto absorbent kitchen paper and apply further colour to the fabric. The

second colour application should slightly overlap the first to produce a two-tone effect.

If required, additional colours can be applied at this stage, although you should make sure that the previous paint application is completely dry before applying a new colour.

If you want to add further paint finishes to the cloth – for example, a stencilled design – you should do it at this stage.

4 Once you are happy with your sponged design, leave the fabric to dry flat. Finally, fix the paints by pressing the reverse of the cloth using a hot iron.

Stencilling

Throughout history, man has employed stencils to decorate everything – from fabrics and furniture to floors and walls. The earliest surviving stencilled design depicts a repeated outline of Buddha and can be seen in the Caves of the Thousand Buddhas in Western China. Dating from the 10th century AD, the Buddha stencils are produced using paper templates and red earth paint.

Perhaps the most prestigious stencilled designs originate from Japan, where stencilling was introduced toward the end of the 8th century. Principally employed as a means of decorating cloth, early Japanese stencils consisted of two layers of paper, identically cut and held together using hair or silk thread. Colour was applied through the stencil – the craftsman had to use enough pressure to produce an image on the fabric, but not so much as to break the fragile paper template or cause the dyes to bleed under the stencil edges. Japanese stencils are often so intricate in design that they appear almost entirely as holes, with very few joins to hold the cut-out elements together. Sometimes the joins of the finest stencils were strengthened with ties of human hair or fine silk thread to keep the design intact. During the 19th century, stencilling was the sole means of producing repeat patterns in Japan and many thousands of exquisite designs were produced on cotton, silk and crepe.

While stencilling was reaching greater and greater heights of sophistication in Japan, the rest of the world slowly began to adopt the technique. However, it was not until the 15th century that stencils were introduced into Europe, where they were employed as a means for overlaying colour onto playing cards and wallpaper. During the 18th century, stencilling spread to America where it was used by colonists as a more economical alternative to hand-blocked wallpaper. Traditionally, stencils were cut from heavy paper stiffened with oil or shellac. Designs included natural forms such as fruit, trees and eagles which were created by combining a

Opposite: Contrasting colourways of the same stencil design. These examples on silk reflect how stencils can be used to decorate large items, such as lengths of furnishing fabric, and small items such as cushions. (Bery Designs)

Left: This design on wool is produced by stencils. While many stencil designs are rigid in appearance, this one is very free in style. (Isobel Messer)

variety of single stencils, each with a separate motif. Paint was applied through the stencils with a brush, while metallic powders were usually rubbed over the surface of the template using the fingertips or a velvet pad. Stencilling reached the height of its popularity in the United States around 1815 when it was employed as a method for patterning walls and floors by itinerant decorators. To begin with, few textiles were decorated using this technique, although with time stencilled fabrics, especially bedspreads, became more commonplace than embroidered ones. Using oil-based pigments, decoration was applied to the cloth in fruit and flower designs.

The late 19th and early 20th centuries saw the introduction of metal stencils or *pochoirs,* especially in France. Produced from zinc or copperplate, these had the advantage over traditional stencils that they were longer-lasting and weren't prone to tearing. Designs were produced by engraving or etching a pattern out of metal and pushing out the central design. Colour could then be applied through the cut-out area in the traditional way.

During the last 20 years, there has been a resurgence of interest in stencilling, particularly in the field of wall and furniture decoration. Certain events have contributed to these modern developments. Perhaps one of the most important reasons for the survival of the craft must be due to the advent of stencil film. Made from transparent acetate, this product allows the stenciller to see not only the piece that he or she is stencilling beneath the stencil sheet, but also any previously stencilled forms, and thus eliminates the need for registration marks. Fast-drying fabric paints, pens and oil-based crayons have also added to the growing popularity of stencilling since they make the work much easier. And photocopiers, with their inbuilt facility for enlargement or reduction, mean that you don't even need to have drawing skills. Simply select an image, change its dimensions on a photocopier, place the photocopy under acetate film and cut out the design using a craft knife.

One of the simplest methods of decorating fabric, stencilling requires little in the way of specialist equipment. If you decide to draw your design freehand onto acetate, you will need to buy a technical drawing pen, although you could use a permanent marker pen instead. If you are planning to cut out a large number of stencils, it may also be worth investing in a cutting mat. This has a self-healing surface that absorbs any cuts and therefore prevents the scalpel blade from dragging across the mat. Cardboard could be used as a base instead, although it is easier to snare the blade in soft cardboard. This not only blunts the blade of the craft knife, but also affects the quality of the result. When selecting a knife for cutting out the template design, it is probably best to buy one with a retractable blade which can be replaced if it becomes blunt.

When choosing a fabric for stencilling, select one with a flat, tight weave since pliable fabrics are liable to stretch, which may smudge the stencil. Most woven fabrics are suitable for stencilling, although if you plan to work with sheers you will need to place a protective cloth underneath your fabric to prevent the colours from smudging. Knitted fabrics are less easy to stencil because of their elasticity. To prevent the fabric from slipping during colour application secure it to the table with masking tape.

You can use stencils to decorate anything from cushions and lampshades to garments. They are also a very popular and inexpensive method for producing borders on curtains and walls. When stencilling ready-made garments, it is important that you place a piece of protective cloth or brown paper between the front and back layers of the fabric to prevent the wet design from bleeding through to the back.

When selecting a fabric paint for stencilling, choose one that is fairly thick in consistency as runny paints tend to bleed underneath the stencil and cause the paint to smudge. A visit to a local craft or hardware store will reveal a whole range of fabric paints that can be used for stencilling. In general, your primary criteria for choosing paint is whether it is suited to the colour of your fabric. For example, if your base fabric is light-coloured, you can work with transparent paints, while if you are working on a dark-coloured background it is better to use an opaque or discharge paint since these prevent the colour of the base fabric from showing through. Paint is applied using a special stencil brush (a stubby brush with short, coarse bristles cut to the same length) or a sponge. There are a number of stencilling kits on the market that are ideal for the beginner.

There are very few rules to remember when working with stencils, although it is worth taking the following into consideration before you begin. Always take up the fabric paint sparingly onto the stencil brush since if too much paint is applied, it is liable to seep under the edges of the stencil. Never stencil with a damp or wet stencil brush as it will cause the edges of the design to blur. Always stamp with an up-and-down motion through the stencil windows and onto the cloth, since normal brush-strokes are liable to distort the template. Once you have completed the first element of your design, leave it to dry before applying the next stencil to prevent the first panel from smudging. Finally, when you have finished stencilling, fix the paints according to the paint manufacturer's instructions.

Right: Inspired by the colours and imagery of India, these cushions are decorated with sponging and stencilling techniques.

The complementary tones of deep blue and terracotta are enriched with splashes of gold. (Ruth Pringle)

how to use stencils

Stencil material is available either as oiled manila paper or clear acetate sheeting, also known as stencil film. While oiled manila paper is the traditional material, acetate has become more popular in recent years. The main advantage of acetate is that it is transparent and therefore enables the stenciller to see through the stencil and onto the fabric beneath. This not only makes it easier for you to align a design, it is also useful if you need to overprint with a second colour.

EQUIPMENT AND
MATERIALS

Fabric

Iron

Paper

Coloured pencils

Masking tape   **Saucer**

Stencil film or acetate   **Sponge**

Permanent marker pen   **Absorbent kitchen paper**

Cutting mat   **Stencil brush**

Scalpel or craft knife

Print table

Fabric paints in assorted colours

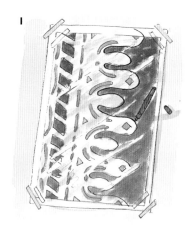
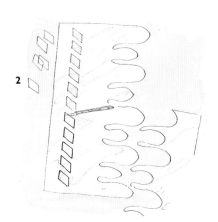
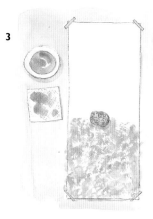

1 As with all painting and dyeing projects, before commencing work make sure that you wash, dry and iron your cloth to remove the manufacturer's finishes.

To make up the stencil, first draw your design to the exact dimensions on paper, making sure that you include sufficient bridges between each shape to hold the design together, then colour in the individual areas with coloured pencils. Tape a piece of stencil film or acetate over your design and, using a permanent marker pen, trace over the outline of the first colour onto the acetate. Repeat this process for the next and subsequent colours, making sure that you use a new piece of acetate for each colourway.

2 Place the first acetate stencil on a cutting mat and tape it securely in place. Next, using a very sharp scalpel or craft knife, cut "windows" out of the acetate where the colour is going to be applied. Repeat this process with each of the subsequent acetate stencils.

3 Using masking tape, secure the corners of your fabric to the print table. Pour a little fabric paint into a saucer, dip the sponge into the paint and blot off any excess on absorbent kitchen paper. Using the paint-charged sponge, apply a pale colourwash over the entire fabric (refer to How to Sponge on pp.62-63 for further information). Leave the cloth to dry flat before applying additional colour.

The most important thing to consider when choosing paint for stencilling is to select a variety that is very dense or thick. This will prevent the colour from seeping underneath the stencil and smudging the fabric beneath. While some paints have been developed specifically for use with stencils, you can employ many ordinary fabric paints for this purpose, providing that they are thick enough. You can even use silk paints as long as you mix them first with a thickener.

Right: This stencil border is highly textured in appearance. The artist has achieved this effect by sponging the background in a pale green colour and then applying a darker shade of fabric paint through a stencil using a sponge. The gold motifs were added afterward using a stencil brush.
(Ruth Pringle)

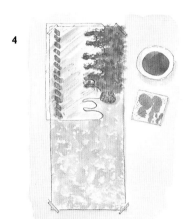

4

5

4 Next, pour a darker shade of fabric paint into a clean saucer and dip a clean, dry sponge into the paint. It is important that you blot off excess paint on absorbent paper at this stage to prevent it from seeping underneath the stencil and spoiling the effect.

Next, place the first stencil on the fabric and hold it firmly in place with your hand. Holding the sponge in your other hand, gently stamp down on the stencil windows using a vertical "dabbing" motion until the colour transfers to the cloth. When you have stamped the sponge dry, dip it into the paint again, dab off surplus paint and continue printing in the same way. When the first pattern is finished, carefully lift off the stencil and wipe the reverse with a damp cloth, then continue printing on the next section of cloth in the same way.

5 To create the gold motifs, fill a clean saucer with gold paint and dip a clean, dry stencil brush into the paint. Holding the "gold" stencil firmly in position with one hand, stamp down on the stencil windows with the brush. When working with stencil brushes, it is important that you use a stamping motion rather than a painting action to prevent colour from bleeding underneath the stencil and producing a jagged outline.

When you are satisfied with your design, leave the fabric to dry, then fix the paints according to the paint manufacturer's instructions.

Marbling

Like many art forms, the origins of marbling are not precisely known, although we have evidence that the Japanese were marbling paper some 700 years ago. According to Japanese legend, marbling was a divine gift, bestowed upon an individual to reward him for his devotion at the Katsuga Shrine. However, other theories suggest that the origins of marbling were contained in a game, played in the Japanese royal court during the 12th century. The game entailed floating paper decorated with *sumi*-ink drawings (a freehand method of marbling) on water, the aim being to capture the inks on the paper.

Throughout history, marbling has been used extensively to decorate paper, the most popular and perhaps most consistent use being for bookbinding. However, in recent years this technique has been developed for use on textiles and today marbling can be employed for patterning everything from furnishing fabrics to accessories. The principle of marbling remains the same for both paper and cloth. It entails floating inks on size (a gelatinous substance) and transferring the resulting designs to cloth or paper. To produce a marbled design, the inks are swirled around using a cocktail stick to form a combed pattern. Many designs have a veined appearance similar to that of real marble, and this is how marbling acquired its name. Finally, the fabric is laid over the patterned ink and lifted off again, bringing a layer of the patterned skin with it.

You can employ a variety of inks for marbling. The classic method involves the use of watercolour paints and size. Carragheen moss, an Irish seaweed, is a typical size and this has been used in the marbling process for centuries. Carragheen moss is available from most health food stores. Other gelatinous substances include methyl cellulose, liquid starch and food gelatin.

If you are a complete beginner to marbling, it is worth experimenting with oil paints before progressing to watercolour paints. Oil paints are very simple to use – first they are thinned with white spirit and then dropped onto the surface of the water.

Left: These silk scarves were marbled using carragheen moss, water and fabric paints. The unusual speckled decoration that results contrasts with the "veined" appearance of traditional marbled cloth.
(Ann Smith)

Right: You can achieve many diverse results using marbling techniques. Because of the random way the inks disperse on water, every marbled item is a one-off.
(Judith Perry)

Many of the conventional marbling processes are time-consuming and laborious to carry out. And, although oil paints and water are straightforward to use, they rarely produce satisfactory results when applied to cloth, the main reason being that oil paints stiffen the material and make it feel harsh. For this reason, you may prefer to experiment with marbling kits before progressing to traditional techniques. These contain everything you will need for marbling cloth, including thickener and marbling

EQUIPMENT AND MATERIALS

Fabric

Marbling bath

Marbling kit, consisting of thickener and marbling inks

Eye-dropper or pipette

Cocktail stick or fine paintbrush

Iron

Rubber gloves

Measuring jug or plastic bucket

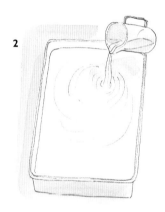

1 First, it is important that you wash your chosen fabric in hot, soapy water to remove any dressing or grease which may affect the material's natural ability to accept the dyes. Next, rinse the cloth in warm water, squeeze out excess moisture and leave to dry. Using a cool iron, press the fabric flat to remove creases.

2 In a measuring jug or plastic bucket, combine one heaped teaspoon of thickening powder with 1 litre (2pints) cold water and leave to stand for one hour.

Pour the resulting mixture into the marbling bath, making sure that the depth of the gel measures at least 3cm-5cm (1½in-2in).

3 Using an eye-dropper or pipette, drop your chosen inks onto the gel. The different colours will float on the surface of the liquid and spread out from the middle of the bath to the edges. Do not drop too much ink as it will sink to the bottom.

4 When the dyebath is completely swamped with colour, create "veined" patterns on the surface of the gel by gently swirling or combing the coloured inks with the tip of a cocktail stick or paintbrush.

5 Once you are happy with your pattern, gently lay the fabric over the inked surface, taking care that the middle of the cloth is the first

inks. The colours are acrylic polymer emulsions and are heat-set. The kit should also contain a pipette which is useful for dropping the colours on the surface of the gel. Marbling kits are available from craft stores and by mail order (see Directory, p.141). When selecting a kit for marbling, bear in mind that the colour intensity will vary between brands, so if you want to achieve a specific result it is worth experimenting with different makes until you find one that you are happy with.

In general, the most suitable fabrics for marbling are those with a fine weave and smooth, even texture. Both will encourage the paints, inks or dyes to bond with the cloth. Fine cottons, linens, silks, rayons and polycottons are all suitable. For this project we have used a variety of materials, including cotton for the ties, and silk for the bow ties and scarf. When you have selected your fabric, check that your marbling tray is wide and long enough to accommodate the cloth without folding.

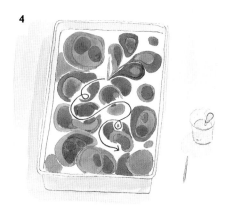

4

5

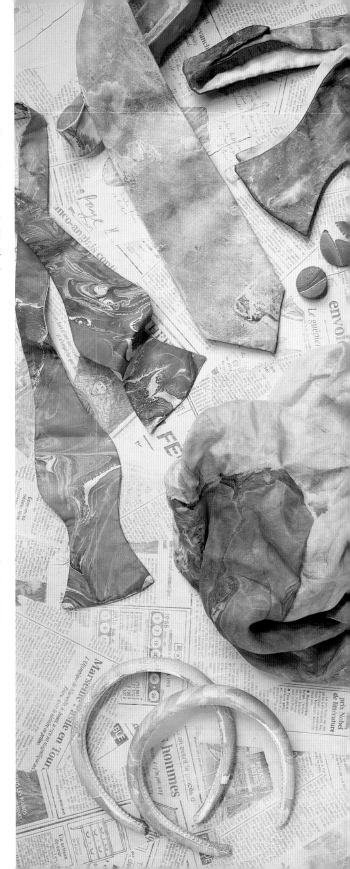

area to come into contact with the medium. Let the edges of the cloth fall into place. Wearing rubber gloves, gently touch the reverse of the cloth with the back of your hand to make sure that the fabric lies flat. Avoid moving the material once it is in position or you are liable to disturb the pattern. Since most fabrics are rendered translucent when they are wet, you should be able to see if any areas of cloth have not taken the pattern. If this is the case, smooth out those areas with the flat of your hand.

When the material has soaked up sufficient colour, carefully lift it off horizontally so as not to disturb the pattern. Next, take the fabric by all four corners and rinse under cool, running water until the cloth loses its slippery feel. Hang the cloth over a clothes line and leave to dry. Finally, fix the paints according to the manufacturer's instructions.

Right: Marbling is an excellent technique for decorating small items, such as these fashion accessories. Included here are cotton and silk bow ties, silk headbands, covered buttons, ties and scarves. The buttons were produced from remnants of marbled silk which the artist used to cover shop-bought button bases.
(Jessica Moxley)

Silk Painting

The Chinese started cultivating silk more than 2600 years before Christ and they were the first people to develop a resist method of embellishing it. Created from rice flour, the resist was applied to the surface of the silk in a linear pattern and then left to dry before flooding the area with colour. As with all resists, the rice flour controlled the flow of the dye on the cloth and separated the areas of colour. With time, this method of painting on silk spread to Japan, which already had a silk industry of its own, where it was employed extensively to decorate kimonos. Popular Japanese motifs included flowers, animals and fish, in particular the chrysanthemum, lotus blossom, deer and crane. The Japanese also developed their resists from steamed rice flour, but they combined it with rice husks, lime and salt. The main ingredient, *mochi* rice, was highly adhesive and not only formed a strong bond on the silk, but also acted as a watertight barrier to the paint. Rice husks were added as a filling ingredient and to counteract the rice's extreme stickiness, making it easier to wash the paste away after use. Lime was employed for its preservative qualities, while salt, being hygroscopic, prevented the paste from drying out during use. The Japanese applied the resist paste through a special stencil, known as a *katagami*, using a thin wooden scraper. The resist barrier was then left to dry before adding colour to the silk by hand.

Opposite: These habutai silk scarves are decorated with acid dyes. (Kerry Shaw)

Left: The artist created "Academia" using mono-printing techniques. This method allowed her to employ an infinite range of colours and textures. Using liquid reactive dyes, she paints onto the surface of a silkscreen, then transfers the colours to silk using water-based gum. (Jackie Guille)

Following these early developments, silk painters worldwide started to research and experiment with new resists in an attempt to find a substance that would allow them to achieve more detailed and painterly results. Probably the most important advancement in the field of silk painting was the discovery of *gutta-percha*, a product of the pallaquium tree. With time, this discovery led to the development of the *gutta-serti* technique. Although there is little documentation about when gutta was first introduced for silk painting, Susan Louise

Moyer writes in her book, *Silk Painting – the Artist's Guide to Gutta and Wax Resist Techniques*, that "during the Bolshevik Revolution, members of the Czar's family dispersed. Many fled to Paris, bringing with them the secrets of silk painting using a substance called gutta, and introduced the process to Western Europe". Later, during the 1920s and 1930s, *gutta-serti* became a popular French craft.

Gutta is to silk painting what lead is to stained glass – it breaks up and contains areas of colour. Gutta is available in applicator or pen form in a variety of different colours, the most popular being black, metallic gold and silver. Glue-like in consistency, it is applied to the silk in a pattern and then left to dry. When it is fully dry, the areas within the gutta barrier are coloured using silk paints. The paint is applied to the cloth using a paintbrush and, due to the absorbency of the silk, it literally flows across the cloth until it reaches the rubbery gutta barrier which contains it. After painting, the dyes are fixed before dry-cleaning the fabric to remove the gutta residue. (If you use coloured gutta, the colour will remain intact after dry-cleaning, even though the process removes the gutta barrier.) Detailed instructions for working with gutta are given on pp.80-81.

The durability, elasticity and lustre of silk make it an unrivalled fibre for fabric decoration. Silk is available in two basic varieties – wild and cultivated – and in many different finishes and weights. When selecting silk for painting, it is best to choose the cultivated variety since this has a smooth, regular surface that evenly absorbs the dye. The main problem with wild silk is that it is unprocessed – i.e. the natural gums and oils have not been removed prior to weaving – and this can inhibit the flow of the dyes across the fabric and produce patchy results. The most suitable cultivated silk for painting is *pongee* or *habutai* silk. Frequently used as lining

Above: A collection of silk-painted shawls, created using the gutta-resist method. Inspired by early 20th-century art, the vibrant colours and innovative designs capture the flavour and panache of that era. (Isaf Designs Ltd)

fabric, this smooth, shiny, tightly woven cloth is available in various thicknesses ranging from five to ten – the higher the number, the thicker the silk. Compared to other fibres, silk is fairly expensive to purchase, but *pongee* is relatively inexpensive and is therefore an ideal cloth to experiment on. Before you begin painting, it is important that you wash the cloth thoroughly in warm, soapy water to remove any special finishes or treatments, or grease, that may repel the dyes and impair the final results. Afterward, rinse the silk and leave it to dry before ironing it flat.

In the step-by-step sequence shown on pp.80-81, I suggest that you use a screen for stretching the silk before you start painting. An adjustable screen or canvas stretcher is useful for this purpose,

although if you are decorating a very large piece of cloth you may need to create your own stretcher by clamping two pieces of wood onto a pair of trestles. If you only intend to decorate a small piece of silk, you could secure it in an embroidery hoop.

Before starting a project, note that the finished size of your work will be the inside measurement of the frame you are using, so make sure that you allow enough material for a seam allowance (if you are making up a garment) or enough fabric to roll the edges (if you are making a scarf). To prevent the dye from seeping into the frame, draw a line around the outer edge of the cloth before applying the paint. When drawing the design in gutta, make sure that the gutta lines are completely solid otherwise the dyes will bleed through the gaps and spoil the design. A good method of checking is to hold the silk up to the light and check that the resist has penetrated through to the back. Once you are happy with your gutta design, leave it to dry for 10 to 20 minutes before attempting to touch it or you are liable to smear the pattern.

When painting on silk using the gutta-resist technique, it is important that you work with special silk dyes (often referred to as silk paints). These should not be confused with ordinary fabric paints which contain binders and extenders to render them opaque. When applied, silk dyes are translucent in colour since they are fully absorbed into the cloth. Their main advantage over fabric paints is that they don't stiffen the silk or affect its luxurious drape or feel.

There are three kinds of silk dyes or paints. The best sort are those that are fixed by steaming. These are available in a spectrum of vibrant colours and are always fully absorbed into the cloth. The second variety of silk paints are those that are fixed in liquid. These are easy to use in the home but the colours are rarely as vibrant as those paints that are fixed by steaming. The third variety of silk paints are fixed by ironing. However, these are not designed to be fully absorbed into the cloth and therefore tend to stiffen the silk and affect its feel. As with most paints and dyes, it is possible to mix colours to create a new shade, providing that you don't combine different brands. Always start with a lighter shade than the one you intend to create, and add a small amount of the darker colour drop by drop until the desired shade is arrived at. If the silk paint becomes too thick during application, simply dilute it with water or alcohol (refer to the manufacturer's instructions for proportions).

Only apply a little paint at one time since a small amount will cover a surprisingly large area of cloth. Don't overload the brush with paint as you are liable to swamp the gutta line. If this does happen — either because the line is broken or because the gutta is not thick enough — repair it immediately. Leave the dyes to dry and then reapply the gutta to both the back and the front of the silk. Finally, using a cotton bud dipped in water or alcohol, dab off any excess dye from the cloth and leave to dry before applying additional paint.

There are a variety of special effects open to you after painting your piece of silk, all of which will achieve different results. If you want to soften the appearance of your painting, simply sponge a little alcohol over the fabric while the dyes are still wet to bleach out areas of the design. For a textured appearance, sprinkle salt crystals over the wet silk. This process produces undulating swirls and shapes, creating light and dark areas on the surface. Once the fabric is dry, you can shake or brush the salt crystals away.

When you have completed your silk painting, it is important that you fix the dyes to make them permanent. The best way to do this is to steam the fabric. This method not only prevents the dyes

from running when they are laundered, but also improves the colour and lustre of the silk. Instructions for steaming silk are give on pp.82-83. After steaming, the fabric can be dry-cleaned to remove gutta residues before rinsing the cloth in clear, lukewarm water to remove excess dyes and restore the cloth's natural lustre.

Above: Heavy-textured silk noil, combined with thick brushstrokes and reactive dyes, lends an extra dimension to the work of this artist. (Helen Harbord)

Overleaf: A fine example of gutta resist. The indigo background contrasts with the bright yellows, oranges, greens and blues of the foliage. (Zoe Phayre-Mudge)

how to use gutta resist

Gutta can be obtained in a disposable tube or with an applicator, either as a clear liquid or with a colour added – such as metallic gold, black or silver. If you are unable to purchase gutta in your preferred shade, it is possible to colour clear gutta in the home by adding a few drops of glass paint to the solution.

Before you begin work, make sure that your gutta is of a workable consistency – if it becomes too thick, add a little gutta solvent to thin it. However, take care not to add too much solvent as this will cause the gutta to bleed uncontrollably

EQUIPMENT AND MATERIALS

Adjustable wooden frame, picture frame or canvas stretcher

Silk fabric

Three-pronged silk pins

Masking tape

Silk paints in assorted colours

Good-quality soft artist's paintbrush

Gutta, gutta solvent and applicator

Paper

Marker pen

Hairdryer (optional)

Iron or fixative

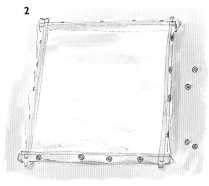

I Using a marker pen, draw your motif to the exact specifications on paper. Make sure that you draw a thick, solid outline around your design so that when you place the paper template underneath the silk fabric in stage 2, the outline is visible through the silk.

Next, gently hand wash the silk in warm, soapy water to eliminate any grease or dressing that has built up on its surface. Rinse thoroughly, roll the fabric in a towel to remove any excess water, then iron it flat while it is still damp.

2 Stretch the silk across an adjustable wooden frame or stretcher and secure it with silk pins or masking tape. (Work from the middle of one side to the corner, then from the middle to the other corner.) Make sure that the silk is pulled taut across the frame, otherwise it will sag and the surface will be difficult to paint.

Place your full-size paper design underneath the silk and use masking tape to fix it to the edges of the underside of the frame.

3 Trace over the design and onto the silk with gutta. Make sure that you apply the gutta evenly and avoid leaving gaps in your design. (If you do leave any gaps, the silk paint will bleed through the gutta barrier and across the fabric

across the surface of the silk, and prevent it from acting as a barrier to the paint. If necessary, practise the technique beforehand on a fabric remnant. When working with gutta, bear in mind that gutta solvent is flammable and toxic, so always work in a well-ventilated room away from naked flames. Store gutta out of reach of children.

After use, it is important that you clean the gutta applicator and nozzle with white spirit to prevent them from becoming blocked. Never leave the gutta in the applicator for more than two days as it is liable to harden. If you don't use all the gutta at the same time, pour any left-overs into a clean glass jam jar. To clean the applicator, turn the tube upside down to allow any remaining gutta to run out and, when the applicator is completely dry, tease out any drops of gutta from the nozzle with a cottonwool bud.

Right: The artist has combined the luxuriant drape of natural silk georgette with a spectrum of pure, translucent colours in order to produce this uniquely sensuous hand-painted scarf.
(Judy Dwyer)

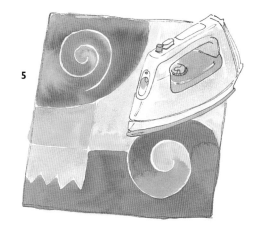

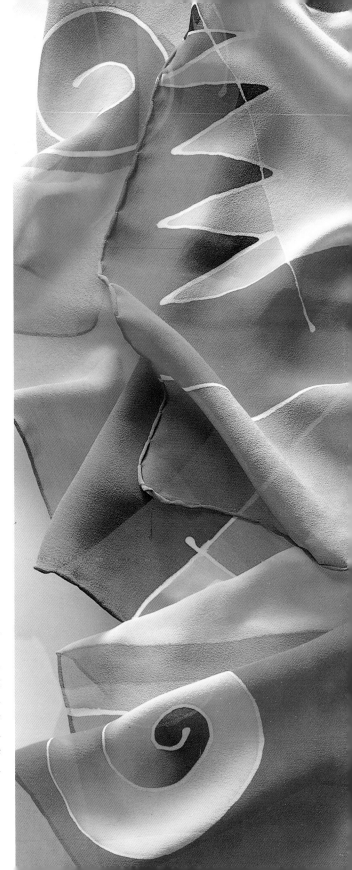

and the colours will become distorted.) To avoid air bubbles in the gutta, up-end the applicator vertically at regular intervals.

Hold the fabric up to the light to make sure that the gutta has penetrated the silk right through to the back (apply more gutta if necessary). Leave the gutta to dry for about an hour (use a hairdryer for speed).

4 Dip a good-quality soft artist's paintbrush into the paint and apply the colour to the silk. Avoid using a painting technique, instead allow the paint to diffuse off the brush and onto the silk. The silk absorbs the colour which runs across the fabric until it reaches the gutta barrier. Make sure that you rinse the paintbrush thoroughly in clean water between each colour application to prevent the colours from smudging and becoming muddy.

5 Once you have completed your design, remove the frame and fix the result according to the paint manufacturer's instructions. This can be done in a variety of ways – from ironing the reverse of the finished piece to dipping it in a proprietary fixative solution. Finally, remove the gutta border by washing the finished fabric in mild detergent.

how to use acid dyes

Unlike silk paints, acid or aniline dyes need to be permanently fixed by steaming to prevent the colours from fading. During the steaming process, the heat and moisture from the steam penetrate to the dyes to produce a concentrated dyebath which bonds the acid dyes to the silk. Professional silk painters employ specialist steamers for this purpose, but these machines are not widely accessible to the amateur silk painter. However, the Directory on p.141 does list a number of craft

EQUIPMENT AND MATERIALS

Acid dyes and binder

Drawing, greaseproof and lining paper

Thick marker pen

Paintbrush

Silk fabric

Print table – table, old blanket and waterproof cloth

Masking tape and strong adhesive tape

Aluminium foil

Pressure cooker

Iron

Glass bowl

Basin of warm, soapy water

Tailor's chalk or soft pencil

Wooden spoon

Rubber gloves

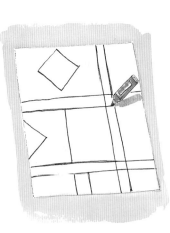

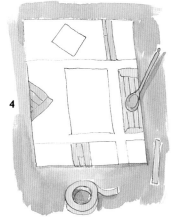

1 Using a thick marker pen, draw a simple design to the exact dimensions on a large sheet of paper.

2 Making sure that you follow the manufacturer's instructions, combine the acid dyes with the binder in a glass bowl. Take extreme care when working with acid dyes – work in a well-ventilated room away from naked flames and wear rubber gloves at all times.

3 To make up the print table, cover a rectangular table with an old blanket, followed by a waterproof cloth – for example, an oil cloth or sheet of PVC lining.

Wash the silk thoroughly in warm, soapy water to remove any grease or dressing. Next, rinse the fabric in clear, running water and leave to dry before ironing flat.

Tape the paper design to the print table, lay the fabric over the top and secure it to the table with masking tape. Using tailor's chalk or a soft pencil, trace the paper design onto the silk.

4 Apply strips of masking tape to the areas of silk that you don't want to absorb the dyes – in this instance, the red background. Push the tape well down onto the fabric with the back of a wooden spoon.

stores and dry-cleaners nationwide with steaming facilities. Large craft outlets should also stock vertical steamers which can be used in the home. Depending on their size, these machines can hold up to 1m (3ft) of fabric. They consist of a double-walled stainless-steel cylinder with a tube inside that rests on a container of water. The steamer is sealed at the top with a dome-shaped lid with a hole in it. Some models are heated using a built-in element, while less expensive models need to be placed on a gas ring or electric hot plate. If you don't want to invest in a special steamer, you can steam small lengths of cloth – for example, a scarf or tie – in a household pressure cooker (see below for instructions). When working with pressure cookers, the main point to bear in mind is to make sure that you roll your painted silk in lining paper before placing it in the machine. This prevents the colourfast areas from rubbing against each other and spoiling the design.

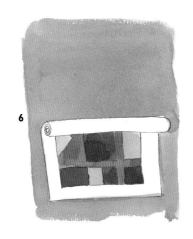

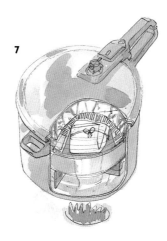

5 Using a paintbrush, paint over the unmasked areas with the acid dye and binder mixture. Leave the silk to dry flat, then apply more tape and colour in the same way. Once you are happy with your design, leave the cloth to dry before fixing the colours.

6 Roll the silk in a sheet of lining paper and flatten and seal the ends with strong adhesive tape. Bend the tube into a neat, tight parcel.

7 To fix the dyes, fill the bottom of a pressure cooker with 2cm (¾in) water. Place the parcel in the basket on the trivet and cover it with greaseproof paper to prevent the fabric from getting wet. Cover the basket with a large piece of aluminium foil to stop any condensation from leaking into the basket. Seal the lid and cook the parcel under pressure for 45 minutes. Leave the pressure cooker to cool, then remove the fabric and leave to dry.

Right: Strong colours and bold shapes are the keynotes of this contemporary artist's work. The bold geometric shapes are created by masking off areas of cloth with tape. The softer features are created afterward using a large artist's paintbrush. (Trisha Needham)

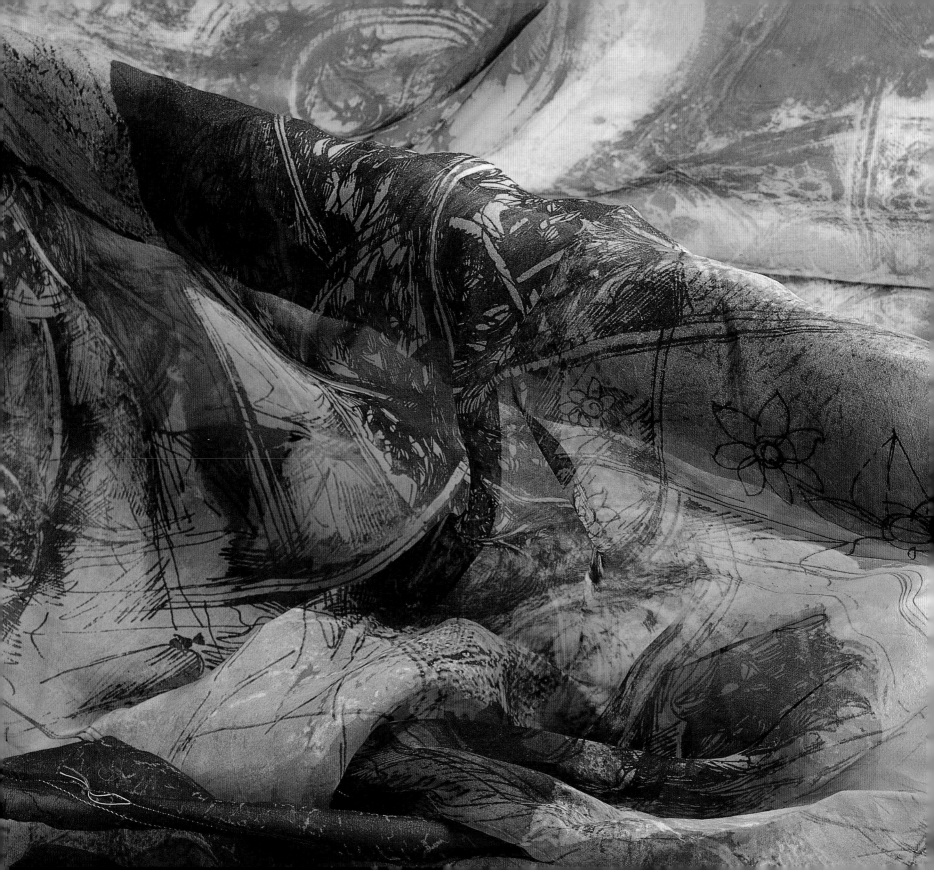

PRINTING

Block Printing

The oldest form of "offset" printing, block printing is a classic method of applying a repeated pattern to fabric. Designs are produced by carving an impression out of a wood or metal block, coating the raised area with ink or paint and firmly pressing the inked block face-down on the fabric. The results are known as block prints.

Although the origins of block printing are uncertain, it is believed that a method of letterpress printing on paper was practised in China and India up to 2,000 years ago. It is equally hard to establish when block printing was first introduced to Europe, although evidence suggests that this method was carried out in German monasteries during the Middle Ages. Early designs consisted of paired animals enclosed in circular shapes, produced using simple cut blocks and black pigments. Block printing was most commonly used to decorate woven garments and hangings.

Traditional methods

While block printing was originally carried out as a craft technique, during the Renaissance this method of fabric decoration started to take off as a commercial venture. Before printing could begin, it was necessary to stiffen the cloth in a solution of parchment scrapings (a by-product of parchment making) and to stretch it taut across a wooden frame. Renaissance blocks were carved from walnut or pear wood, and each one usually measured a

Previous page: Silkscreen-printed cloth.
(Jessica Trotman)

Above: These silk organza scarves are decorated in a tulip design using block-printing techniques.
(Lin Knott)

Opposite: Block-printed silk scarves. To create the waterlily design, the artist painted the cloth with a print paste before block printing using discharge pastes (see Discharge Printing, pp.92-97).
(Lin Knott)

quarter the size of the frame. The printer transferred the pigment from the carved block to the cloth by rubbing the material against the carved, inked block from below, using a small wooden board. Traditionally, only undyed fabrics were printed in this manner although later, when it became possible to produce rich colour effects, it was more common to dye the fabric in a contrasting colour before printing. Occasionally details were hand painted or stencilled afterward.

In 1791, calico printer Charles O'Brien wrote the *British Manufacturer's Companion and Callico Printer's Assistant*, the first book of its kind to be produced in England. In it, he states that "Blocks should not be above nine inches [23cm] long, it being handier for working and not so apt to warp... and for very close fine prints that are difficult to join, the smaller are the better". O'Brien included instructions on all aspects of block printing – from making a block to adding pitch pins for registration purposes and preparing the cloth ready for printing. It is no wonder that at the end of the 18th century block prints were being produced throughout Europe to such a high standard.

At the turn of the 19th century, roller printing started to overtake block printing in popularity and by 1840 roller printing dominated the English textile-printing industry. However, during the 1870s William Morris, the leader of the Arts and Crafts Movement, attempted to redress this imbalance. Morris's passionate desire to revive the industry made block printing fashionable once again. Choosing to ignore so-called progress in the field of textile decoration, Morris revived traditional block-printing techniques, believing that block-printed designs were far superior to roller-printed ones. As with his printing, William Morris also chose to ignore recent developments in the field of chemical dyeing. Enlisting the help of dyer Thomas Wardle, Morris reintroduced vegetable dyes, taking his recipes from old books and herbals. Both processes were more costly than the technologies that replaced them, so the revival was limited to those who could afford to pay for the superior quality.

Toward the middle of the 19th century, cast or stereotype blocks were introduced in France. Although this method of printing caused some deterioration in detail, cast blocks gradually improved in quality and today they are employed almost exclusively in the production of fine line and detail block prints, particularly for discharge work. Their main advantage over wood is that they are less expensive to manufacture.

Modern techniques

Today, the most popular woods for block making are sycamore, box, lime and pear. To produce a block, several layers of wood are glued together so that their grains run in different directions. Next, a pattern is transferred to the block using carbon paper. The areas that need to be carved are then tinted with watercolour paint and chiselled away to a depth of $\frac{1}{4}$in to $\frac{3}{4}$in (1cm-2cm), depending on the type of fabric you are printing. The next stage involves filling the carved-out hollow areas with thick felt soaked in gum. Felt is used because it is highly absorbent. The wood is then sealed with varnish to make the block waterproof and hardwearing. Finally, two finger grips are created in the back of the block to facilitate handling and pins are inserted into the corners for positioning purposes. Known as pitch pins, these are designed to print a small precise dot on the cloth which can be used to determine the positioning of subsequent blocks. The finished block is then coated with paint or ink and printed on the cloth. With each print, the printer strikes the block with the wooden handle of a printer's maul or mallet. By hitting the block in this way, the weight is distributed evenly over the surface of the block, thus giving an even print. When the first colour print has dried, the second colour is applied using a new block in the same way. The second block is registered by following the pitch marks from the previous block. Thus, an image is built up layer by layer and colour by colour.

Although wood is still employed for making blocks, it is difficult to carve wood in the home without specialist skills and equipment. Today, a more popular material is lino which is simpler to carve than wood but just as hardwearing. The step-by-step sequence overleaf provides instructions for making a lino block and reveals how to apply the pattern to fabric. It also includes useful advice on selecting paints and inks for block printing.

Perhaps the most familiar type of block print is the potato cut. Although not as sophisticated as wooden blocks or lino cuts, potato blocks are ideal for producing simple patterns on cloth or paper. To make a potato block, simply cut a potato in half and carve out a design in relief from the smooth, cut surface using a sharp knife. Often the best designs are the simplest to produce – for example, a single stripe which can be printed in any direction to produce stripes, chevrons or squares. Once you are happy with your carved design, it is important that you blot the potato on a piece of absorbent paper to remove excess starch and moisture. Finally, dip the block in a saucer of ink or paint and press it firmly onto the fabric. You can carve a number of different mediums in this way – lino floor coverings, bottle corks or even erasers. To create a design from an eraser, draw a simple pattern on the surface with a soft pencil and cut out the resulting areas with a sharp craft knife or scalpel, making sure that you angle the sides. Avoid cutting deep incisions in the surface of the eraser as these may weaken it and cause it to break up. To create a patchwork effect, combine a variety of different shapes and designs on one length of fabric.

Another exciting method of creating block prints is to glue or nail objects to a piece of wood. For example, to create a swirling pattern, coil a length of string or cord into a design and secure it to a piece of wood with permanent glue; while for a spotted design, hammer large-headed tacks or nails into wood so that when you print they produce a polka-dot effect. Any object with a textured or raised surface can be used in this way. However, if your object is very small (such as a button or a coin), it is a good idea to glue it first to a piece of wood or a matchbox to facilitate handling.

Obviously some people prefer to buy blocks rather than making their own. You can buy block-printing kits from craft stores and by mail order (see Directory, p.141, for suppliers). These are available in a variety of styles and contain everything you need for block printing, including the block, roller and paint or ink.

how to make a block print

You can make a block for printing from a variety of different mediums. While this design is created using lino, you could use a potato block to produce a simple motif – such as a spot or stripe. To do this, simply cut a potato in half and carve a design in relief out of the flat edge. Before you dip the potato block in ink or paint, wipe off excess moisture or starch on absorbent paper other-wise your result will look watery.

Traditionally blocks were cut from wood, but you may find it easier to use lino instead as this is easier to carve, providing you have specialist cutting

EQUIPMENT AND MATERIALS

Cotton fabric	**Tracing paper**
Wood for making the block and pad	**Masking tape**
Plastic sheeting	**Coloured marker pens**
Old blanket	**Ruler**
Strong glue	**Dish or dyebath**
Lino	**Iron**
Lino-cutting tools	**Drawing pins**
Blue and black fabric paints	**Hammer and nails**
Soft pencil	
Paper	

I Draw a design to the exact proportions on paper and colour in the various areas using coloured marker pens. Using a pencil and tracing paper, trace off each colourway onto a separate sheet of tracing paper. For example, for this design there are two colourways (black and blue) so you will need to do two tracings.

2 Place each sheet of tracing paper face-down on a separate piece of lino and, using a soft pencil, rub over the reverse of each design so that the pencil pattern transfers to the lino. Remove the tracing paper, taking care not to smudge the image. Using lino tools, cut out the designs in relief, i.e. you will need to cut out the areas surrounding your pencil design so that the pencil markings stand out in relief.

To make a block, cut out a piece of flat wood to the same dimensions as your lino, then nail a narrow piece of wood to the reverse to act as a handle. Using strong glue, stick the lino onto the flat side of the block and leave to dry.

3 To make a print table, cover a smooth, oblong table with an old blanket and plastic sheeting. Next, wash your fabric in hot, soapy water, rinse and leave to dry. When the fabric is completely dry, iron it flat and tape it to the prepared table.

tools. Once carved, the lino is mounted onto a hand-sized piece of wood to facilitate handling.

When working with block prints, it is important that you apply the paint or ink evenly to the surface of the block otherwise a patchy design will result. It is a good idea to make a dye pad for this purpose. This consists of a piece of wood covered in absorbent material. The pad is dipped into the ink so that it absorbs the dye and then pressed against the block so that the paint transfers to the block.

The main point to consider when choosing paints for printing is that their consistency is thick enough to be transferred from the block to the cloth. If the ink is too thin, the design is liable to smudge and the paint will drip across the the fabric. For best effects, the ink or paint should be the consistency of wallpaper paste. If you are unable to find a paint of the right consistency, add a thickening agent to an existing colour until the correct consistency is arrived at.

Right: This geometric design is produced in two colourways using lino block prints. (Camberwell College of Arts)

Using a soft pencil and a ruler, mark out a grid on the fabric, showing where the block should be placed each time for printing. (Each grid square should be the same size as your lino block.)

To make a dye pad, take a separate piece of wood, making sure that it is larger than your print block, and cover it with plastic sheeting. Secure the plastic to the wood on the reverse with drawing pins. Next, cover the plastic with a piece of blanket and secure this with pins in the same way. Pour the blue fabric paint into a dish and press the dye pad into the paint. Once the dye pad has absorbed the paint, remove it from the dish and press it against the first printing block so that the lino picks up an even layer of paint.

4 Lay the inked block on one of the grid squares and apply a firm pressure so that the design transfers to the cloth. Gently lift off the block, checking that the print has registered, then apply more ink to the block and place it on an alternate grid square. Continue printing in this way until you achieve the desired effect, then leave the cloth to dry. Apply the second block and black paint. Once you are happy with your design, leave the fabric to dry flat and fix the paints according to the manufacturer's instructions.

Discharge Printing

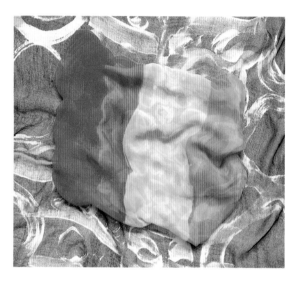

Most textile paints, especially those manufactured for domestic use, are not suited to printing on dark-coloured fabrics. The reason for this is that the background colour tends to show through, which makes the paint look muddy and dull. Although you can decorate dark grounds using opaque paints, these have the disadvantage that they are not absorbed into the fabric like transparent paints and therefore make the cloth feel harsh and stiff.

The best method of printing on dark-coloured fabric is a process known as discharge printing. The traditional method of producing a discharge print involves chemically bleaching out, or "discharging", a pattern from a piece of dyed cloth and subsequently reprinting the bleached areas in a new colour. Today the bleaching and colouring processes can be carried out simultaneously using a range of special dyes. These are mixed with a discharge paste and, when applied to the fabric, bleach out a pattern and deposit a new colour in its place.

Traditional techniques

One of the first individuals to carry out discharge printing successfully was a Scotsman called Monteith, who in 1802 developed the "Monteith process", a direct method of applying chlorine to dyed fabrics. The process involved sandwiching a length of turkey-red fabric between two thick cast-lead plates decorated with perforated patterns. A bleaching agent was poured onto the upper plate and this filtered through the perforations onto the lower plate. Because the plates were so tightly clamped together, the pattern was controlled. Thus, when the fabric was removed and washed in cold water, the areas that had come into contact with the bleaching agent became white or off-white, while the unbleached areas remained turkey red. One of the most common designs that Monteith produced was a dot motif. The red-and-white spotted textiles that he created were made into men's handkerchiefs, known as "bandannas" due to their likeness to the traditional Indian tie-dye methods of decorating cloth (see p.38).

Left: These silk chiffon scarves were hand painted using discharge dyes. (Kerry Shaw)

Right: The joy of working with discharge paste is that you can produce strong, rich colours. This artist has combined subdued autumnal tones with vivacious tropical shades to produce an exclusive range of wool scarves. (Noreen Conwell)

94 printing

It was Daniel Koechlin, a Frenchman, who made the most significant developments in the field of discharge printing. He produced his first samples of red-and-white patterned cloth by overprinting the red cloth with a solution of strong tartaric acid, which he immersed briefly in a solution of chloride of lime. This process resulted in a chemical reaction – when combined, the two chemicals released hydrochloric acid which discharged the background colour. Another important discovery made by Koechlin was that it was not possible to bleach the colouring agent Prussian blue using acidulated chloride of lime. As a result of this discovery, Koechlin was able to produce a design in three colourways – red, white and blue – by adding Prussian blue dissolved in acetic acid to the print, which resisted the acidulated chloride of lime.

Many other experiments have taken place in this field, although some were less scientific in their approach than others. During the 1930s Phyllis Barron and Dorothy Larcher discovered a method of discharge printing. This involved dipping a French block decorated with a small flower and geometric design into nitric acid and block printing the acid onto indigo-dyed fabric. More recently, Susan Bosence developed a method of discharge printing using citric acid discharge on potassium permanganate fabric (see Glossary, p.138). Bosence combined the potassium permanganate with a thickener to form a paste and used it to hand print or block print onto indigo-dyed cloth. The main drawback of her method was that she was only able to store the permanganate paste in a stable condition for short periods of time, and thus was only able to use her method to produce small lengths of cloth.

Left: This silk crepe de chine scarf combines discharge printing
techniques with hand dyeing.
(Sacha Denby)

Modern methods

Although discharge printing was developed almost 200 years ago, this method of decorating cloth is still unpredictable. For this reason, it is important that you make notes of the quantities and dyes that you use and keep samples of your results.

Although discharge printing is considered to be less predictable than conventional printing, it does have advantages over direct printing. Firstly, discharge printing enables you to overprint a light, bright colour onto a dark or black background; secondly, it enables you to print fine, intricate patterns; and thirdly, discharge prints are not affected by spoiling, which does occur with direct printing when a design overlaps.

In order to make a discharge print, you must first dye the cloth with a discharge dyestuff – i.e. a dye that can be removed by bleaching. These are reducible dyes and are available in many different colours and forms, including direct, acid, reactive and disperse dyes. Manufacturers grade discharge dyes from one to five for their dischargeability. If you want to produce a white discharge, you will need to use a number five discharge dye. However, if you are printing a coloured discharge, you will not require perfect dischargeability and can therefore make do with a lower number, such as three or four. Because of the unpredictability of this technique, it is a good idea to experiment with different grades of discharge dye on a fabric remnant before starting a project.

Before use, you should mix your discharge dyes with a reducing agent, which is designed to withdraw oxygen or add hydrogen to other substances. There are two reducing agents in current use: stannous chloride and sulphoxylate (which is stablized with formhaldehyde). While stannous chloride (tin salt or tin crystals) is the traditional agent, today it is more common to use sulphoxylate as this causes less damage to the cloth and equipment. Note: sulphoxylate decomposes at temperatures above 80°C (176°F), so you should avoid drying your discharged cloth at high temperatures. As with all chemicals, it is important that you handle reducing agents with care. Wear rubber gloves when making up the print paste and work in a well-ventilated room away from naked flames. Store stannous chloride and sulphoxylate in an airtight container away from heat and dry conditions, and keep them out of reach of children.

As with all printing processes, it is important that you combine your dye with a thickening agent to prevent the colour from bleeding uncontrollably across the cloth. You should always add the thickening agent to the paste at the last possible moment in order to prevent the discharge dyes from destabilizing. When you choose from the variety of thickening agents, make sure that you select one that is not affected by your reducing agent. Traditional thickening agents for discharge printing include gum arabic and gum tragacanth.

Once the discharge paste is complete, you can apply it to fabric in a variety of different ways. The step-by-step project on pp.96-97 provides instructions for applying discharge paste through a silkscreen. However, you could apply the paste through a stencil or via a block print. Other techniques involve applying the paste with a paintbrush, squeegee or sponge.

As with most techniques, once you have completed your textile design it is important that you fix the colours to prevent them from fading. The traditional method for fixing discharge prints involves steaming the cloth, although some artists have achieved successful results using a household steam iron. For further information on fixing discharge dyes, refer to the paint manufacturer's instructions.

how to make a discharge print

Before dyeing your cloth, you must first weigh it to establish how much discharge dye you require. If you want to colour the fabric black, the dye should weigh 10 percent of the weight of your fabric – i.e. if the cloth weighs 100g (3.53oz), you will need 10g (0.35oz) of dye. (For paler shades, you will need 1 to 2 percent.) Measure the glouber salts in the same way – these should weigh 10 to 40 percent of the weight of the cloth. Because the salts are added in stages to the dyebath, the quantity will depend on how long it takes to reach your desired colour.

EQUIPMENT AND MATERIALS

Habutai silk fabric

Dischargeable acid dye

Glouber salts

Wetting agent

Print table (see p.90)

Masking tape

Batik wax

Silkscreen

Squeegee

Steamer

Measuring jug

Mixing bowl

Bain-marie or melting pot

Measuring scales

Wooden spoon

Decorator's brushes in assorted sizes

Safety mask

Iron

For coloured discharge paste: 3g (0.1oz) illuminating acid dye; 2g (0.07oz) Glyzine A; 20cc hot water; 60g (2.12oz) Printel; and 15g (0.53oz) Formasul

For clear discharge paste: 60g (2.12oz) Printel; 25g (0.88oz) hot water; and 15g (0.53oz) Formasul

1a

1b

2

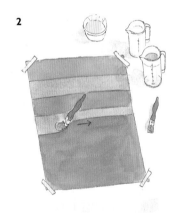

1a/b Before you start to print, you must first dye your cloth using a dischargeable acid dye (see above for instructions).

Next, melt the batik wax in a bain-marie or melting pot. Dip a 2.5cm-5cm (1- or 2-in) decorator's brush into the wax and paint stripes across the surface of the silkscreen. Leave the wax to set and cool.

With the iron on a low setting, press the dyed silk, then tape it to the print table.

2 Note: for the next stage, you will need to work in a well-ventilated area and cover your face with a protective mask.

To produce a coloured discharge paste, combine the illuminating acid dye powder with the Glyzine A in a measuring jug. Add the hot water by degrees and mix to a smooth paste with a wooden spoon. Leave to cool. When the mixture is completely cold, add the Printel and powdered Formasul. Weigh the resulting paste. If the mixture weighs less than 100g (3.53oz), make it up to that weight by adding extra Printel to thicken or more hot water to thin the mixture (depending on the texture of the paste). The final viscosity of the discharge paste should be that of wallpaper paste.

Fill a dyebath with hot water. Again, the amount of water is based on the weight of your cloth. The water should weigh between 30 and 40 percent of the weight of the cloth. The cloth needs to be fully immersed in water, so choose a vessel that is deep enough to accommodate the fabric.

Dissolve the dye in a little water. Place the dyebath on a gas or electric hob and bring the water to simmering point. Pour the dye into the dyebath and stir well. In a separate dyebath, dilute the wetting agent with water (see manufacturer's instructions)

and immerse the cloth. Next, place the wet cloth in the dyebath and stir with a wooden spoon to encourage the cloth to absorb the dye evenly. Remove the cloth after five minutes and add a handful of glouber salts. Put the fabric back in the dyebath and stir for a further five minutes before removing the fabric and adding another handful of glouber salts. Continue in this way until the desired colour is arrived at. Note: the fabric should remain in the dyebath for at least an hour. Finally, remove the fabric, rinse in cold water and leave to dry.

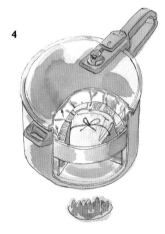

To produce a clear paste, combine the Printel with the hot water and Formasul and mix to a paste. Again, the mixture should resemble wallpaper paste, so if it is too thick add a little extra water, while if it is too thin add more Printel. Using all or some of the colours, paint stripes or blocks of colour onto the silk with a decorator's brush. Leave to dry.

3 Pour the clear paste into the waxed screen and, using a squeegee, print over the wax-painted brushstrokes.

4 Dry the silk, then steam the cloth in order to fix the dyes (refer to How to Use Acid Dyes

on pp.82-83 for instructions). Note: because the dyes are unstable the fabric should be steamed within four hours of applying the dye.

Rinse the fabric in cold water and then wash it in warm, soapy water. Rinse it again in cold water and leave to dry.

Right: These silk scarves were produced using a silkscreen and discharge paste, as described and illustrated here. The artist begins by painting the screen using molten batik wax. This process produces a textured, resist effect on the cloth.
(Bronwen Hargreaves)

Transfer Printing

One of the most recent developments in the field of textile printing, transfer or "sublistatic" printing involves the use of heat to transfer patterns from paper to synthetic fabrics. A special paper web is painted with "dispersed" dyestuffs which sublime at a temperature of between 71°C and 104°C (160-220°F). (Sublimation is the chemical conversion of a solid substance into a vapour by means of heat – on cooling, the substance resolidifies.) Thus, when the transfer paper is placed in contact with the fabric and heated to that temperature, the pattern is transferred from the paper to the fabric. Heat transfer has two distinct advantages over silkscreen printing: it is a speedy process – printing times vary from 15 to 45 seconds – and because the dyestuff is automatically fixed when it comes into contact with heat, this method is suitable for decorating stretch fabrics that might otherwise be distorted during the finishing stages.

Although transfer printing is a relatively recent development, it is similar in principle to the method used for transferring embroidery designs onto fabric, which has been in existence for more than a century. The main developments in the field of transfer printing took place from 1950 onward. In 1952, ICI took out a patent for a sublimation technique, but on discovering that it could not work commercially allowed it to lapse. Then in 1960, Noel Deplasse started experimenting with the technique and, on finding that ICI's patents had lapsed, started to use the technique commercially in France. In 1970, Bemrose, an old English printing company, became involved in the transfer-printing business using their own patents and by 1984 they were exporting transfer paper as far afield as China.

Opposite and Left: These transfer-printed garments form part of the artist's "Turbo Boost" collection. The shiny lycra and waterproof nylon capture the surface quality of the subjects – motorbikes and cars of the 1990s. Transfer printing gives the artist great flexibility – here she produces large- and small-scale designs with a free, expressive style. (Kate Gibbs)

Fabrics

Originally, it was only possible to transfer print onto fabrics that contained a high percentage of

Above and Right: This collection of transfer-printed lycra swimwear was influenced by sea life. The design is first painted onto transfer paper using special dyes and then transferred onto fabric using a heat press. (Zoe Lewis)

polyester – the higher the better for clarity and colour – although later it became possible to print onto other synthetic fibres, including acrylic, acetate, triacetate and Nylon 6.6. However, recent developments enable you to use this technique for printing onto woven fabrics with a 30 percent natural fibre mix.

During the 1970s, following growing dissatisfaction with nylon and polyester fabrics and a move back to natural fibres, scientists began experimenting with transfer printing natural fibres. In recent years, work has progressed into the field of transfer printing wool, silk, cotton, viscose, suede and leather. This progression has been made possible by a method known as "wet transfer" which is carried out using Fastran®, a trade name given to the viscose paste used in this type of printing. Although more elaborate than conventional heat-transfer printing, wet transfer is currently growing in appeal.

Wet-transfer printing involves four processes: first the cloth is padded using a viscose paste made from Fastran® powder, then it is passed through a mangle before printing with reactive, rather than disperse, dyes. The dyes remain in contact with the fabric for between four and six minutes, after which time the cloth is scoured and milled. Although this method involves more processes than dry-transfer printing, wet-transfer printing is fairly straightforward to carry out – it requires care rather than special skills on the part of the operators. However, because this method is still in its early stages of development, at present it is not possible to carry out wet-transfer printing domestically.

Practicalities

For the student or amateur, heat-transfer printing does have its advantages – for example, when producing multi-coloured designs it isn't necessary to make up a screen, while for silkscreen printing you would need to produce a separate silkscreen for each colourway. Another advantage is that the only preparatory work involves drawing a design and tracing it onto paper, which gives the designer much more freedom of expression and design. And because the patterns are produced directly on paper, it is possible to reproduce almost any design in this way, since you are not reliant on the cloth's ability to accept certain paint effects. Finally, since all the colours are printed in a single operation, transfer printing saves time and expense and means that there is less chance for misregistration in the design, which frequently occurs during conventional printing.

Unlike silkscreen printing, transfer printing is not limited to printing lengths of cloth. You can use this technique for decorating areas of garments or even entire items of clothing. Transfer printing is even suitable for decorating knitted garments and accessories, especially hosiery. A trip to a local department store will reveal a vast array of garments and accessories that have been printed in this manner. These include tee-shirts, babies' clothes, nightdresses, swimsuits, leotards, tights, socks and even ribbons. This method of decoration has also taken off in the field of advertising, since it is a fast and efficient means of transferring cartoon characters and company logos to tee-shirts, baseball caps and jackets.

However, transfer printing is not limited to commercial purposes only. Instructions for making a transfer print in the home are given on pp.102-103. As you will see, this method of textile decoration requires very little in the way of specialist equipment. All you need is a piece of synthetic fabric, domestic transfer paints and brushes, special transfer paper (see p.141 for suppliers) and an ordinary household iron for transferring the design onto cloth.

how to make a transfer print

This method of decoration is only suited to patterning synthetic fabrics, such as polyester, nylon, lycra or acrylic. Transfer printing is best used where you wish to produce an intricate multi-coloured design on cloth. In fact, it is the only method of printing different colours simultaneously. Transfer printing can be employed to pattern both finished garments and lengths of fabric. The main advantage of decorating clothing in this manner is that the finish doesn't fade during machine washing. The only point to bear in mind when decorating made-up garments is that you must place a piece of thick paper between the front and back to prevent the

EQUIPMENT AND MATERIALS

Synthetic fabric

Paper

Marker pens in various colours

Masking tape

Layout paper

Transfer pens, paints and crayons in assorted colours

Paintbrushes

Iron

Newsprint

I Using coloured marker pens, draw your design on paper to the exact specifications. Choose shades that are as close as possible to the transfer paints you intend to use. If you don't have the exact colours, indicate where they should go using a pencil. Tape your paper design onto a work surface and, using masking tape, secure a piece of layout paper over the top.

2 Using your original design for reference, trace over the pattern with coloured transfer pens, paints or crayons. Use the paint or ink directly

from the pot and wash the paintbrush frequently to prevent the colours from becoming muddy. Leave the design to dry thoroughly.

3 Crinkle up a large piece of newsprint and tape it onto a work surface using masking tape. Iron the fabric flat and then tape it over the newsprint. The crinkled paper will give your final design added texture and depth.

4 Place the decorated layout paper face-down on the fabric and secure the corners with masking tape.

coloured paints from transferring through both layers during the heat-transfer process.

Transfer printing is very economical to carry out. In fact, you can use the same paper design over and over again until the design fades beyond recognition. The only stage that needs special care is the heat-transfer process itself, since if you move the cloth or paper while it is being ironed you will smudge the design.

When applied to paper, transfer paints are very dull in appearance and this can be misleading since they are in fact very vibrant when transferred to cloth. If you are in doubt as to the final colour, it is worth testing different shades on a remnant of fabric before starting a project. To give your design extra depth, place textured objects such as shells or rope under the layout paper and rub over them with wax transfer crayons to create a textured effect. You can then transfer the embossed pattern to the cloth in the normal way.

Transfers are available as paints, inks or crayons from craft stores. Unlike many fabric-painting techniques, you can mix different brands of transfer paint and use pencils and crayons simultaneously.

3

4

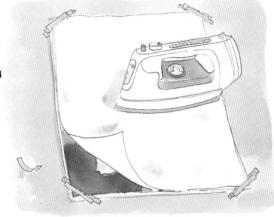

Set the iron on a medium heat and carefully iron the paper from top to bottom. Make sure that the paper doesn't slip as you transfer the pattern since this will result in a smudged design.

Finally, lift off one corner of the paper to make sure that the pattern has transferred to the cloth. If it has, carefully peel back the transfer paper. If not, repeat the heat-transfer process. Unlike ordinary fabric paints, there is no need to fix transfer paints because they are automatically fixed during the ironing process.

Right: This fluid design displays fish and sea - horses in vivid shades of blue, yellow and green. The joy of working with transfer paints and pens is that you can create free, painterly images, which are very true to the original design. This free approach is rarely *achieved when working with other printing techniques. (Zoe Lewis)*

Silkscreen Printing

A development of stencilling, silkscreen printing is based on techniques developed in Japan during the 8th century. Although primitive in comparison to modern screen printing, early Japanese methods involved cutting open designs in papyrus or lacquer-stiffened paper and applying the colour through the cut-out portions of the stencil with a brush. The main drawback of this technique was that, when large areas of fabric needed to be printed, ties were necessary to join the individual stencil shapes together. The advantage of silkscreen printing is that these ties are not required.

When silkscreen printing was first developed, it was carried out entirely by hand. The process involved stretching a piece of fine silk organdie across a frame and forcing ink or paint through the taut surface of the silk onto the cloth beneath. To produce a picture, the screen was converted into a stencil by masking or blocking off areas of the silkscreen to prevent the ink from passing through those areas onto the fabric below. Today, masking or blocking can be carried out in a variety of ways – from painting a varnish onto the screen in a pattern to cutting out a design from clear adhesive film or cartridge paper and sandwiching this against the screen (as shown on pp.112-113). However, in this book the method that has been used most consistently for silkscreen printing involves the use of a photosensitive emulsion.

Above: The artist combined an expanding medium with metallic and standard ink to create this silkscreen print. The expanding medium creates a three-dimensional effect on the cloth.
(Michelle Blomley)

Right: These silk crepe de chine and georgette scarves were created using hand-painting and silkscreen-printing techniques. The artist employed a variety of mediums, including acid dyes and discharge paste.
(Sophie Williams)

Today, hand printing is still carried out along traditional lines. First the frame is placed over a piece of fabric, then a thick-textured dye is forced through the exposed mesh of the frame using a rubber scraper (a squeegee). Usually two people are required for this process – one person holds the screen in position and the second pushes the dye through the screen using a squeegee. Once the first area of fabric is printed, the frame is carefully lifted off, so as not to smudge the design, and moved to the next section of cloth to repeat the pattern using the same colour. When the first colour is dry, the process is repeated using a new shade and a second screen. (A separate screen is required for each colour separation.) Because the mesh of the screen is so fine, when the dyes are pushed through the frame the joins are invisible. You can reproduce any picture in this way, providing that you draw the design on the screen beforehand. Hand printing revolutionized the textile and fashion industry for this reason. While block printing was time-consuming and meant that only small areas of fabric could be printed at one time, silkscreen printing was inexpensive and enabled large areas of fabric to be decorated at once. This had a dramatic influence on the fashion world. While block printing limited the designer's scope to small geometric repeats, with silkscreen printing came the opportunity to produce free, painterly designs in strong colours.

In the step-by-step sequence on pp.112-113 the simplest method of stretching mesh across a frame is explained. A design is produced on cloth by masking or blocking off areas of the frame using a paper stencil which is fixed inside the screen using heavy-duty tape. While this method is easy to carry out at home, it is not suitable for multi-printing and will not produce the same results as those achieved in a factory or workshop.

Many of the fabrics in this chapter have been produced using a method known as photo-silkscreen printing. Although it is based on simple hand-printing techniques, this process involves the use of a photosensitive emulsion and a darkroom. First, the screen is degreased using a solution of ammonium bichromate. (Always refer to the manufacturer's instructions when working with chemicals since the percentages of ammonium and photosensitive emulsion vary according to the brand.) Next, the screen is coated with a photosensitive emulsion. To do this, first tilt the screen at a slight angle and then force the emulsion up the screen from the base to the top using a squeegee or soft, flat brush. It is important that you carry out this process in subdued lighting since, although liquid emulsion is not light-sensitive when it is wet, as it dries it will begin to sensitize. Leave the screen to dry in a darkroom at a temperature not exceeding 30°C (86°F). When the front of the screen is dry, apply a coating of emulsion to the reverse side of the screen in the darkroom. Depending on the brand of photosensitive emulsion you are using, you can leave the photosensitized screen in a darkroom for up to three months before exposing it under a lightbox.

To produce a design, first draw each colour element of your pattern on paper and then trace them onto Kodatrace (transparent film) using an opaque ink or paint which will not allow light through when the screen is exposed. Make sure that you draw the design on the matte, non-slippery side of the film. To transfer your design to the screen, place the Kodatrace against the screen, making sure that firm contact is made by pressing it flat with a plate of glass or suction device. Next, expose the screen to light under a lightbox for 2-25 minutes, depending on the kind of exposing cabinet or lightbox you are using. In this way, the areas that are covered by opaque ink are not exposed and will wash off, leaving the open mesh of the screen through which the colour is applied. Immediately after exposure, wash the screen in warm water (55-65°C/131-149°F). It is best to do this in a sink or bath by spraying the screen with a shower attachment. This process clears away any unwanted photolayer from the unexposed parts of the mesh. Wash the screen quickly as the exposed areas of the screen are delicate at this stage and could peel off if they are exposed to water for too long. The screen then needs to be left to dry at a temperature not exceeding 30°C (86°F). Once it is fully dry, examine the screen for faults and pinholes and

mend these with resist paint. Before printing commences, make sure that you reinforce the inner edges of the screen with brown sticky paper (as shown on p.113) and seal this with varnish to make the edges fully watertight.

Equipment and materials

A visit to a local craft or hardware store will reveal a large variety of purpose-made fabric paints that are suitable for silkscreen printing. These are usually ready-to-use (they have already been mixed with a binder) and are normally fixed by ironing the back of the cloth. Fabric paints are available in opaque or transparent finishes, depending on the feel and

Right: The artist used an identical screen to produce the gold background for these cushions. The red cushion is embellished with a third colour, applied through a second silkscreen.
(Cressida Bell)

finish you require. If you intend to print on a dark-coloured background, it is best to work with opaque paints. These are thicker than the transparent variety and are designed to sit on the surface of the fabric. Their main disadvantage is that they affect the drape of the cloth and make it feel stiff. Transparent fabric paints, on the other hand, are more suitable for printing on light-coloured backgrounds as they are actually absorbed into the fabric. You can also buy fluorescent, pearl or glitter paints for silkscreen printing. However, these are more expensive than conventional paints, so you may find it more economical to apply them with a paintbrush after you have finished printing.

Most fabrics are suitable for screen printing, although different materials will react to the paints in diverse ways. Those with a flat, even weave will produce an image close to the original design, while textured cloth tends to produce a less uniform result. When printing on sheer fabrics, it is important that you place a backing cloth under the fabric to absorb some of the paint and prevent it from bleeding onto the print table. When working with heavyweight cloth, such as piles and furnishing fabrics, you will need to apply more printing ink than for sheer fabrics.

Although the step-by-step sequence on pp.112-113 requires very little in the way of specialist equipment, one indispensable tool is a squeegee. This is employed to force the ink or paint through the screen onto the fabric. When purchasing a squeegee, make sure that the rubber edge is perfectly true, since irregularities cause uneven printing and poor results.

While silkscreen printing was originally carried out using a frame made from pure silk, today it is more common to use a synthetic mesh frame, such as fine terylene or nylon. If you plan to print using photo-silkscreen methods, it is probably best to

employ a monofilament screen. The main disadvantage of working with a multifilament screen is that the print paste is inclined to stick to the fibrous surface and become clogged in the mesh. Finally, before you begin printing make sure that your print table or work surface is completely flat, since a warped table will produce patchy, uneven results. Instructions for making up a print table are given on p.82.

Opposite: This sample of cotton furnishing fabric has a strong, graphic feel. The artist designs with large dimensions in mind, namely ceiling-to-floor curtains and huge sofas. (Michael Walker)

Above: Everyday objects, including a screw, a safety pin, a pair of scissors, a hand, a clock and working diagrams of machinery, are combined in this unusual silkscreen composition on wool. (Victoria Bond)

how to make a silkscreen print

If you are a complete beginner, it is worth practising this technique on calico or cheap lining material before progressing to expensive fabrics. When drawing your design, start off with a single-colour print and then build up to using two or more colours. If you decide to use more than one colour, bear in mind that when the colours overlap on the fabric they will produce a third colour. Thus from a red, blue and yellow design you can also create orange, purple and green.

EQUIPMENT AND MATERIALS

Coloured pencils

Paper

Tracing paper

Soft pencil (4B)

Cartridge paper	**Print table**
Masking tape	**Iron**
Cutting mat	**Fabric**
Craft knife or scalpel	**Fabric paints or inks**
For the frame: terylene or nylon mesh; wooden frame; staple gun; brown gummed paper tape; polyurethane varnish and paintbrush	**Squeegee**

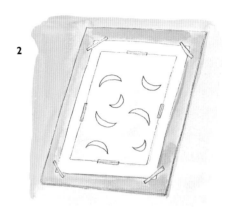

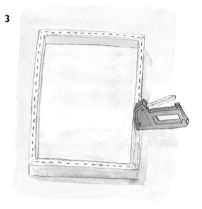

1 Using coloured pencils, draw your design to the exact specifications on plain paper.

2 Place a piece of tracing paper over your design and, using a soft pencil (4B), trace off each element onto a separate sheet of paper. For example, to produce this design you will need to do two tracings – one for the moons and one for the stars.

Take a piece of cartridge paper 5cm (2in) larger than the size of the drawing and secure it to a cutting mat with masking tape. Place one of the tracings face-down on top and trace the design through to the cartridge paper. Remove the tracing paper. Next, using a craft knife or scalpel, cut windows out of the cartridge paper where the colours are to be printed. Make up a second paper stencil in the same manner using a fresh piece of cartridge paper and the second design.

3 To make the screen, cut a piece of terylene or nylon mesh 10cm (4in) longer than the frame. Place the mesh over the frame and fold the raw edges inward. Starting in the middle of one side, staple the mesh to the frame at regular intervals until you reach the corner. Next, starting in the middle of the same side, staple outward toward the other corner. Take care to keep the mesh taut at all times. Next, staple the opposite side in the same manner then repeat this process for the other two sides. Wash the screen ready for printing and leave to dry overnight.

If you don't want to make up a frame from scratch like we have done, it is possible to buy ready-made frames from craft stores. These are available in a variety of fibres to suit your needs. When choosing a frame for screen printing, make sure that you select one with a flat base, since a warped frame will result in an uneven print. While wooden frames are the least expensive, if you plan to do a lot of printing you may want to invest in the metal variety.

Previous page: This collection of one-off accessories was hand painted and printed directly onto silk. The artist is inspired by the process of ageing and the aesthetics of decay. (Neil Bottle)

Right: The artist employed a variety of techniques to produce this scarf. First, she dyed the silk in a vibrant shade, then she painted the borders and finally she applied the moons and stars through silkscreens. (Trisha Needham)

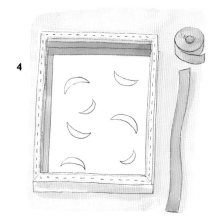

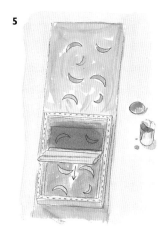

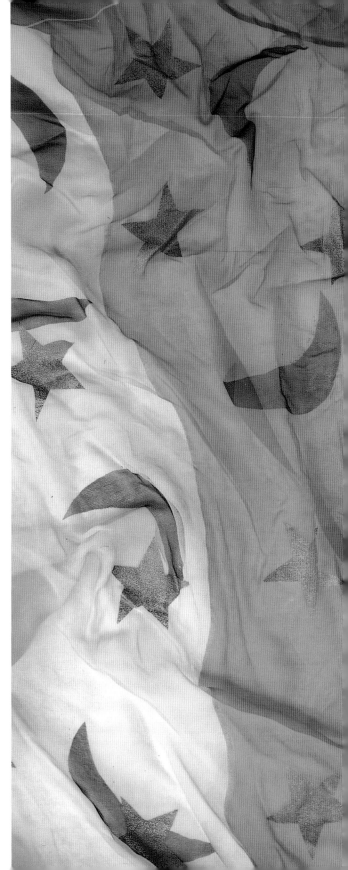

4 Place the screen face-down on a table and insert the "moon" stencil inside. Dip a length of brown adhesive-backed paper tape in water, squeeze out excess moisture, then wrap the damp tape round the inside of the screen so that the tape covers the edge of the paper and the sides of the screen. Leave the tape to dry, then turn the screen over and apply more tape round the edges of the face of the screen. This process will prevent the ink from seeping under the stencil (step 5) and spoiling the design. Leave the tape to dry, then paint over it with polyurethane varnish to seal completely.

5 Iron and tape the fabric to the print table, then position the screen on the cloth. Holding the screen firmly with one hand, pour the blue ink along one end of the screen. Put the squeegee behind the ink and, tilting the squeegee toward you, pull it firmly across the screen. Carefully lift off the screen, checking that the print has registered, then place it on the next area of cloth and continue printing in the same way.

While the first colour is drying, make up another screen using the "star" stencil and a clean silkscreen. Place the prepared screen on the cloth, making sure that you align the pattern, and print the second colour in the same manner as the first. When you are happy with your design, leave the cloth to dry flat before fixing the inks according to the manufacturer's instructions.

When a piece of cloth is silkscreen-printed with a pigment or a dye, you also need to use a vehicle for applying the dye in the form of a paste. This is often referred to as a thickening agent and is designed to increase the viscosity of the dye to prevent it from spreading across the screen and, at the same time, make it possible to apply a controlled amount of dye to the fabric. Manutex printing is an unusual method of silkscreen printing in that instead of the dye being mixed with the thickening agent and then

EQUIPMENT AND MATERIALS

For the frame: wooden frame; monofilament terylene or nylon; staple gun; brown gummed paper tape

Tree bark, wood, shells or leaves

Silk noil or dupion fabric

Wax fabric crayons

Manutex powder

Procion M or reactive dyes

Wooden spoon

Plastic vessel

Jam jars

Ruler

Paintbrushes

Squeegee

Print table (see p.82)

G-clamps

Iron

Masking tape

I To make the frame, stretch a piece of mono-filament terylene or nylon mesh over a wooden frame and staple it securely to the edges to form a smooth, taut surface (see p.112). Cover the inner sides of the frame with brown gummed paper tape to seal the frame and prevent the manutex from seeping out through the sides.

2 Place the screen face-down on the tree bark, wood or shells and, applying a firm pressure, rub through the screen with a large wax fabric crayon. This process causes the textured surface to be transferred to the surface of the screen. Make sure that you apply the wax very thickly as

it tends to wear away during the printing process. For added interest, lay other textured materials such as dried leaves under the screen and rub over them vigorously with wax fabric crayons in the same manner.

3 Following the manufacturer's instructions, mix the dyes with water in individual jam jars. Place a clean paintbrush in each jar of dye.

Turn the screen face-up and, using the dye mixture, paint a design on the top of the screen. Leave to dry.

4 Set the iron to a silk setting and press the fabric. Secure the cloth to the print table with

applied, the dye alone is painted directly onto the screen. When the dye has dried, the thickening agent (manutex) is then pulled across the screen with a squeegee to make the print.

This method of printing is not suited to making evenly coloured repeat prints since, with each pull of the squeegee, the dye on the screen becomes increasingly faint. If you do wish to produce multiple prints, make sure that you apply additional dye to the screen after each pull of the squeegee.

When constructing the screen for printing in this way, it is important that you select a fine-gauge monofilament nylon or terylene mesh since the dye is prone to bleed through an ordinary multifilament screen.

The most suitable dyes for making manutex prints are Procion M or reactive cold-water dyes, which can be fixed by ironing. Procion H dyes may also be used, but these are fixed by steaming. These dyes are available from craft stores (see p.141).

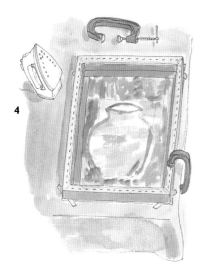

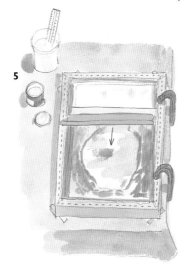

masking tape. Place the screen face-down on top of the fabric, then secure it to the table with G-clamps to prevent it from slipping.

5 Measure out 4 tsp (20ml) manutex and tip it into a clean jam jar. Pour 1 pt (500ml) of cold water into a straight-sided plastic vessel and stir the liquid vigorously with a ruler to create a vortex. Tip the manutex into the vortex and, as the powder comes into contact with the water, start stirring in the opposite direction. Continue stirring until the liquid forms a thick, smooth paste.

Transfer the mixture to the screen and, following the instructions given on pp.113, print using a

squeegee. When you are satisfied with your design, leave the fabric to dry.

Finally, fix the dyes according the the manufacturer's instructions.

Right: In order to give her work extra depth and texture, this innovative artist has developed a method for painting a wax resist onto the screen before printing with manutex. Using large wax crayons, she rubs through the silkscreen onto textured surfaces such as wood, tree bark, leaves or shells to create an embossed, "frottage" effect.
(Caroline Bailey)

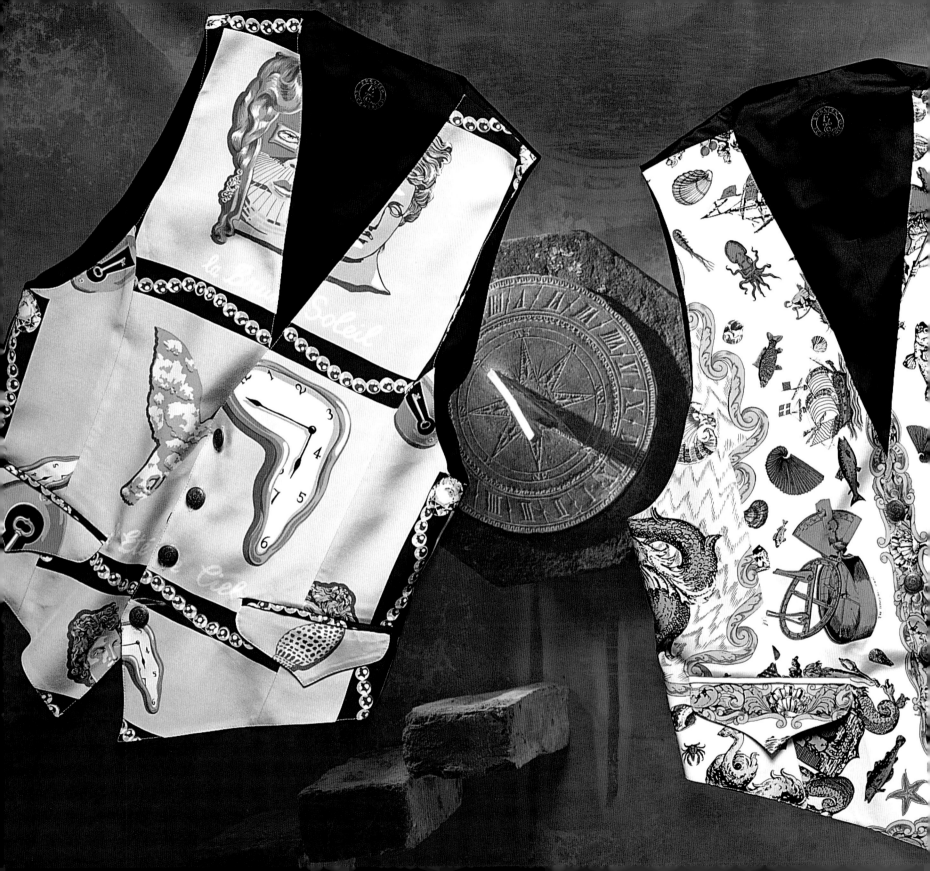

CLOTHING

Clothing

Clothes that you once loved but have since become tired of can be given a new lease of life at little expense with new and exciting decorative treatments. The same is true of newly bought items. Plain ties, scarves and tee-shirts can all be transformed from standard items into unique pieces with the addition of a little paint or dye. In this section, you will find garments and accessories that have been decorated using all manner of techniques – from hand painting and dyeing to silkscreen printing and discharge painting. While the earlier chapters provide instructions for carrying out these techniques, this chapter reveals some of the special effects you can achieve by combining different finishes on clothing and accessories.

Tee-shirts are a good starting point for beginners since they are inexpensive to purchase and can be decorated using many of the techniques featured in this book. If you prefer to practise on a small area, ties or scarves are a good alternative. For the complete beginner, specialist kits are available which contain everything you will need for decoration, including fabric paints or dyes and a scarf or tie (see Directory, p.141, for suppliers).

Before beginning work on a new garment, it is important that you wash and iron it in order to remove any dressing which could prevent the paint or dye from being properly absorbed into the cloth. This will also prevent further shrinkage. The

Previous page: The printed waistcoat on the left is influenced by surrealist art, while the one in the middle is based on sea themes. The silk waistcoat on the right, with its cherubs and clouds, has a whimsical feel.
(English Eccentrics)

Above: This sophisticated silk overshirt is discharge printed with a classic blue-and-white spot.
(Osbourne Rose Prints)

Right: These velvet hats are hand painted in rich colours.
(Anna Steiner)

same is true of existing garments. Make sure that you wash and iron them thoroughly, so the cloth is clean and free from grease. Depending on your preferred method of decoration, you may also need to remove items like buttons or zip fasteners as these may distort the results. For example, it would be virtually impossible to stencil over a button, press stud or snap fastener since the stencil wouldn't be able to lie flat. Finally, since most garments have a front and a back, it is important that you place a barrier between the two layers to prevent the dye or pigment from passing through from one side to the next. Brown paper or cardboard is ideal for this purpose.

If you are working on a ready-made garment, you may find it easiest to draw your design in tailor's chalk first. If you are printing or stencilling, it is best to use your pattern over a large, flat area such as the back of a dressing gown or the base of a skirt. Avoid decorating uneven surfaces, such as where a gathered sleeve meets an armhole, since this will produce uneven results. If you are using the transfer method of printing (see pp.98-103), make sure that you cut the transfer paper to the size and shape of the garment you are decorating. This will help you when you come to iron your design in place and will yield even results. The same is true of stencils. If you are making the stencil from scratch, it is best to cut it to the same dimensions as the piece of work you are stencilling — for example, a cuff or a collar — so that you mask off all the cloth you want to remain free of paint.

If you are good at dressmaking, you will probably decide to make your garment up from scratch using a paper pattern or the equivalent. If this is the approach you decide to take, it is worth considering decorating the pieces of cloth after you have cut them out but prior to making up. This method is particularly useful if you want to match up a design

along the seams or if you plan to add special details to pockets or cuffs. The main point to bear in mind if you decide on this approach is to make sure that you take into account the seam allowances. For example, if you are matching a design down a seam, make sure that part of the pattern isn't lost in the seam allowance when the garment is made up. Before you start painting, mark the seamline with tailor's chalk and make sure that your design doesn't extend beyond that line.

Choosing a design

Before you start to paint, you will have to decide what your subject is going to be. While artistic people generally choose to create their own one-off designs, if you are not good at drawing there's nothing wrong with basing your design on an existing pattern. The Design Sources chapter is filled with ideas for patterning fabric and explains some of the different approaches you can take (see pp.28-33). If you decide to copy a design from an existing pattern, all you need to do is find your source material — you may choose to reproduce a pattern from a piece of wallpaper or a book illustration. Once you've settled on your design, simply trace off the pattern you want to reproduce using embroidery tracing paper and transfer it onto fabric. If your source material is too large or small for your chosen garment, you can enlarge it on a photocopier. Simply place the illustration on the copy-glass screen and adjust the size using the zoom button.

Opposite: These silk accessories were produced using the discharge-printing method. You can create vivid colours using this technique without affecting the cloth's natural drape. (Tessuti)

Right: This classic dressing gown is decorated with a spectrum of rich colours, including purple, blue, green and gold. It is padded then lined with silk for added warmth. (Osbourne Rose Prints)

Right: These silkscreen-printed garments display a sophisticated combination of colour and texture. The silk shirt was created from a patchwork of different fabrics in a variety of colourways. (Pazuki Prints)

Opposite: These scarves in slipper satin and crepe de chine were decorated using discharge dyes. The richness and depth of colour was achieved by over-dyeing and reprinting using a limited range of colours. (Victoria Richards)

Of course, you don't have to limit yourself to representational designs. Instead of painting or printing, why not employ a technique that will to a large extent dictate the result? For example, sponging and spattering do not require drawing skills nor does tie-dyeing or marbling, although they do require time and patience. The same is true of stencilling. You can buy stencilling kits from craft stores, and these contain everything you will need for decorating a garment or accessory (see Directory, p.141, for a list of suppliers).

A good starting point for any fabric designer is to draw inspiration from an existing garment. For example, you may have a favourite dress or a printed shirt that you like and want to use as a basis for your own design. Simply pick out some of the elements from the original print and use them to create a new pattern – you could, say, enlarge them or even employ them in a less formal way. If you are drawn to the colour combination of an existing outfit, why not pick out and reproduce those colours for your own design? Alternatively, pull together a few elements from existing outfits to create a new garment. For example, create a range of accessories using motifs from a printed skirt and colours from a shirt or jacket. Accessories are a good way of tying together a new outfit. They might include any or all of the following: bag, gloves, shoes, cummerbund, scarf, shawl, tie, hat, collar, cuffs or buttons. Because accessories are generally small in size, they are often a good way of using up remnants of decorated cloth that you might otherwise throw away. Buttons, in particular, are simple to make and look wonderful when applied to a plain jacket or velvet waistcoat. You can buy buttons for covering from haberdashery stores and they are available in many sizes to suit your needs. A similar product is available in earring button form. These too can be covered in your chosen fabric.

Right: Inspired by the strong colours and rhythms of Africa, these sumptuous silk-satin scarves are silkscreen printed in rich shades of gold and blue. (Cressida Bell)

The way in which a fabric falls has a tremendous influence on the final appearance of a garment and should be taken into consideration before you begin painting or printing. Whether the design is to be worn closely fitted to the body, as in a leotard, or loosely draped across the shoulders, as in a stole, will dictate the way in which the design is seen. For example, if a garment is stretched across the body, the fabric and design will be thinner and more translucent in appearance. So, if you are patterning tights or stockings your design will take on a transparent look when it is stretched over the leg, while if you are decorating fabric for a full, gathered skirt, the design will seem more opaque in comparison. The same is true of colour and texture. Japanese fashion designer Issey Miyake uses the texture of his fabric as the starting point for all his fashion designs: "Borrowing the easy and adaptable attributes of the kimono makes it possible to appreciate the beauty of both the fabric and the human body, and, in addition, the harmony that can be created when both are allowed expression."

When you are designing for a specific garment or accessory, bear in mind the style and shape of the item. For example, while some items of clothing look good when they are decorated with an all-over design, others may be swamped by it. For an unusual effect, experiment with decorating focal areas of a plain garment, such as the pockets, cuffs or collar of a white shirt. Long areas of material, like the skirt of a full-length overcoat or dressing gown, are generally able to take a large-scale design, whereas the same effect might look ridiculous when used to decorate a hat, glove or mini dress.

In the past, the fashion maxim was never to mix prints. However, this rule has been overthrown by many of today's designers. Neil Bottle (see pp.110-111) and Pazuki Prints (see p.122) both

126 clothing

mix prints to great effect. The prints may be connected by a single colour or they may even be complete opposites. For example, soft stripes and Fair Isle patterns can look good together. Some of the world's greatest contemporary fashion designers – such as Kenzo and Ungaro – have made their names by mixing florals, plaids and stripes with abandon. During the 1980s, John Leflin, the design director of Liberty department store in Regent Street, London, England, introduced a fresh, contemporary approach to his designs by mixing checks, tartans, plains and the traditional – but ever popular – floral prints.

One interesting method of translating designs to fabric is a technique employed by knitwear designer Kaffe Fassett. When I attended one of his lectures, he projected slides of his knitwear designs onto a woman wearing a white shirt in order to see exactly what his designs would look like when they were translated into garments. He chose a wide variety of themes for the experiment – from complete scenes such as a beach covered with seashells, to shelves of books and rows of brightly coloured vegetables in a marketplace. By taking slides of your own designs, you could carry out this same experiment and reflect your design ideas onto a selected fabric to see if they translate well onto cloth.

Care of fabrics

The main factor to consider when choosing textiles for clothing and accessories is whether they can be laundered. The same is true of your chosen decorative technique. It's not worth spending time and money creating a specially painted, printed or dyed garment, only to find out that you are unable to fix the paints and it is therefore impossible to wash or dry-clean it. Laundering instructions vary according to the fabric and brand of paint that you employ, but in general it is best to wash delicate items, such as fine silk scarves, by hand using a mild detergent, especially those with special finishes such as heat-expanding, metallic or glitter paints. Any fabric that is likely to shed dye should be washed separately in cold water. However, avoid immersing the cloth in water for any length of time since this might encourage the colour to fade. A final word of warning: avoid laundering hand-dyed fabric in biological washing powder because the colours are liable to run. If you are in doubt as to the best laundering procedure, take your garment, together with the paint or dye you employed, to a specialist cleaner and follow their advice.

Opposite: The edges of these silk georgette scarves are silkscreen-printed to produce crisp blocks of colour. These contrast with the hand-painted sunflower motifs that decorate the middle and corners.
(Donna Read)

Above: These silk ties and scarves are decorated with sunflowers, leaves and other natural forms. The artist was influenced by the textile design of the 1950s, although she employs the subtle shades of the 1990s.
(Victoria Richards)

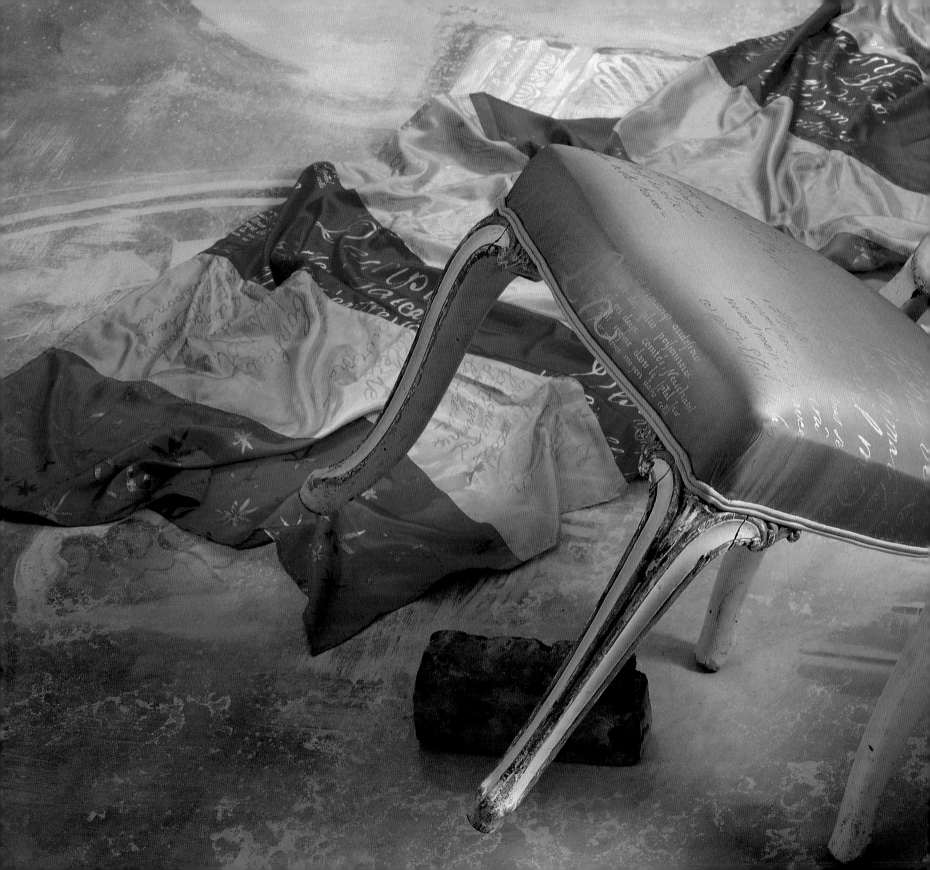

INTERIORS

Interiors

When planning a design for furnishing fabric, it is important that you consider the proportions of your room. For example, do you want to create a feeling of space or are you aiming for a cozy atmosphere? Since it is normal to design and paint on a flat, horizontal surface, you may find that when your finished fabric is folded, tucked or draped it looks completely different. Therefore, you must establish what you are going to make before beginning work. If you are unable to pre-visualize the final effect, it might be worth painting a sample section of fabric and putting it in position to see if it looks and feels right.

Furnishing fabrics

A wide variety of textiles can be employed for soft furnishings. In general, your choice will be determined by the article you are making and its function in the home. Curtains, cushions, floor coverings and loose covers all require specific fabrics, so it is worth seeking advice before making your choice. For example, if you are decorating fabric for loose covers you will require a cloth that can stand up to constant wear-and-tear, such as a linen union, while if you are making bedlinen you will need a light, comfortable material that is easily laundered and soft to the touch, such as a poly-cotton. When you have settled on a suitable weave and weight, make sure that the cloth is either washable or dry-cleanable. If you are unable to wash or dry-clean it, find out whether you can use a proprietary fabric protector to prevent staining. Finally, you will need to make sure that your choice of textile paint or dye is suitable for your project. Is it colourfast? Is it suited to decorating large areas of cloth? Will it fade after continued exposure to light? How do you fix the dye? All these points are important and you should find the appropriate answers in the paint manufacturer's instruction leaflet. One final point to consider: if you are decorating upholstery fabric, find out whether it can be treated with a fire retardant. This can be obtained from theatrical suppliers and some hardware merchants.

Previous page: These chairs are decorated using a variety of mark-making techniques, including screen printing and hand painting. (Carolyn Quartermaine)

Left: An original alternative to shop-bought accessories, these colourful lampshades were hand-painted using a stunning assortment of colours. (Cressida Bell)

Right: Decorated using silkscreen-printing and hand-painting techniques, these brightly coloured cushions have a strong geometric feel. (Anne-Marie Cadman)

Left: These unique chairs are decorated with stylized images of peace and love. They were produced on linen and silk using silkscreen printing and hand-painting techniques.
(Carolyn Quartermaine)

Curtains

Windows are focal points in rooms so it is important that you think carefully about what you use to decorate them. Because a window allows you to show off your fabric over a large area, a curtain project is an excellent opportunity to make the most of your creative flair and imagination. However, before you let your imagination run wild take a close look at the proportions of your room – your window dressings should complement, rather than obscure, its style and size. In general, small motifs such as a simple geometrics are more adaptable than large, pictorial designs. If you do settle for a bold, pictorial pattern, make sure that you choose a curtain or blind that shows off the design to its full extent. Like traditional *toiles de Jouy,* modern pictorial prints are best used flat in order to appreciate the full value of the design. For this reason, it is probably best to limit their use to plain curtains or roller blinds, all of which will display patterns to full effect.

Roller blinds are good for beginners because they are stiff and easy to work on. Blinds can be decorated using many of the techniques described in this book – including hand painting, stencilling and silkscreen printing – and using a variety of fabric paints, including crayons, opaque paints and fabric pens. Because blinds are large and bulky, the most efficient method of fixing the paints and dyes is to blow them with a hairdryer six inches (15cm) from the surface. After installation, they can be cleaned periodically using a hand-held vacuum cleaner or duster.

The variety of fabrics available for making curtains is enormous. In general, natural fibres are most suited to this purpose since they absorb the dyes readily and tend to hang, drape and feel better than their synthetic equivalents. One important point to bear in mind when decorating textiles

for curtains or blinds is that the design will fade if it is exposed to light for long durations. With curtains, the easiest way to prevent undue fading is to line and interline them. Not only will this protect the fabric, the extra weight will also encourage them to hang better. Cotton sateen is often employed for lining curtains since it is hardwearing and drapes well. It also has a shiny outer surface which helps resist dust and dirt. However, if you don't want the formality of fully lined curtains and prefer to work with sheer fabrics such as natural calico, it's worth experimenting with vat dyes since

Above: This parchment-coloured cushion is decorated with medieval illumination using silk-screen printing and hand painting.
(Bettina Mitchell)

*Right: Two felt wall-
hangings are decorated in
co-ordinating colours
using discharge-printing
techniques.
(Harriet Benson)*

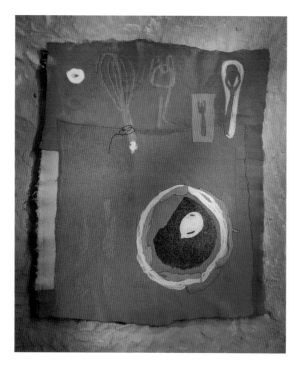

*Right: The artist hand-
painted this floorcloth
using oil paints, then
sealed the finish for durability using varnish.
(Natalie Woolf)*

these are colour- and lightfast (see p.25 for more information on vat dyes). You can learn more about the vat-dyeing process by attending a workshop (see p.141 for a list of addresses).

When decorating a large area of fabric, it is important that you find an appropriate surface on which to work. I have hand-stencilled floor-length curtains by laying them on a floor covered with newspaper. However, make sure that you have a helper if you plan to do this, since you will need someone to help you to manipulate the cloth and move it to a suitable place for drying. Fixing is often a problem when decorating a large piece of fabric and for this reason it is important that you consider the fixing method before you start work. While most paint and dye manufacturers state the appropriate fixing instructions on their product, it is often impossible to carry out their recommended

techniques successfully on a large expanse of cloth. For example, the most popular method of fixing, and one that has been employed extensively throughout this book, is to press the reverse of the fabric for five minutes using a hot iron setting. However, if you need to fix a pair of floor-length curtains, this method would prove too slow and laborious. For this reason, it might be worth checking with the paint or dye manufacturer to see if it is possible to fix the paints or dyes using another technique. A quick and efficient method is to blow the cloth with a hairdryer. Steaming is another popular method for fixing cloth and is widely used for finishing discharge-printed items and hand-painted silks. If you don't have steaming facilities at home, make enquiries at local dry-cleaners and colleges, which may be equipped with a large, industrial-sized steamer.

Wallhangings and floorcoverings

Sparsely decorated rooms can be changed beyond recognition by pinning or stapling hand-decorated textiles to walls or by covering uneven floorboards or ugly, worn carpets with printed, stencilled or painted cloths. A wallhanging or floorcloth is the textile equivalent of a painting and will allow you to give free range to your imagination. You can employ a number of different techniques when decorating floorcloths or wallhangings and, because they don't need to be joined together like curtains or loose covers, there is no need to allow for repeats in the design.

Natalie Woolf produces bold, one-off designs for floorcloths by hand painting with oils on canvas. Her inspirations are varied and include anything from natural forms to kitchen implements. Once her painted design is complete, she seals the

canvas with layers of durable varnish to protect the surface and make it hardwearing. As a result, her floorcloths are easy to clean – all you need to do is sponge them with warm, soapy water. If you are not confident enough to draw a design freehand, you could achieve excellent results using block printing or stencilling techniques.

Harriet Benson also produces large-scale designs in bright colours, but she employs a completely different medium. Her wallhangings are crafted from felt which she decorates using silkscreen-printing, pigment-dyeing and discharge-printing techniques. Benson's inspirations are varied. At present her work is influenced by kitchen utensils. Working on felt gives her images depth, as well as softening the edges of what would otherwise be hard-edged shapes. And because felt doesn't fray like ordinary woven cloth, one of the main advantages of employing it for soft furnishings is that you don't have to hem the edges. Another benefit of using felt for wallhangings is that it will greatly improve your insulation, as well as acting as an excellent soundproofing device. The texture and weight of felt also make it an excellent fabric for scatter rugs, since it is both hardwearing and soft underfoot.

Pete Shaw is another textile artist who produces large, one-off designs. "The scale of the hangings is obviously important as is the scale of the imagery used. They must stand up to close scrutiny, especially if they are hung at floor level. They must have enough visual information to hold the viewer's interest at close quarters but not so much information that it becomes unreadable from a distance – they must work both ways." Shaw uses a combination of dyes and pigments in his work and applies them using a variety of tools – including rollers, brushes, sponges, screens and lino-cut blocks (see p.59).

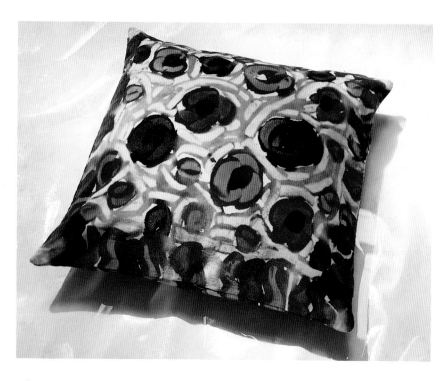

Above: The artist hand-painted this velvet cushion cover using discharge dyes and thick brush-strokes in order to achieve a strong painterly quality. (Donna Read)

Opposite: The central panel of this bedcover is decorated with a cockerel design using silkscreen-printing techniques. The sides are embellished with a rich garland of golden leaves and finished with rosettes. (Osbourne Rose Prints)

Bedlinen

Like windows, floors and walls, the bed is another large, flat expanse and therefore an excellent area on which to display your hand-painted or printed textiles. Duvet covers, valances, sheets, pillowcases, bolsters and eiderdowns may all be decorated using any of the techniques featured in this book.

The main criteria for selecting fabric for bedlinen is to choose a soft and comfortable material, with some ability to resist creasing for ease of laundering. As an alternative to making your own bedlinen, you could decorate ready-made items. However, if you decide to do this, make sure that you place a piece of cardboard or thick paper between the two layers of a duvet cover or pillowcase to prevent the paint from seeping through to the other layer.

Accessories

A screen is an excellent opportunity to show off textiles that you have created yourself. Both sides can be covered identically or with different fabrics – perhaps a bold pictorial subject on one side and a simple stripe or polka dot on the reverse – so that you can change the emphasis of the room with your mood. Free-standing screens are highly versatile – if you have an unsightly fireplace you could place a screen around it to conceal it, or if you live in a large studio apartment you could employ screens to divide the room into different living areas.

Cushions are an ideal project for beginners since they are small in scale, easy to handle and inexpensive to produce. Almost any fabric can be made up into a cushion cover and you can use any of the techniques featured in this book to decorate it – from sponging and stencilling to hand painting and silkscreen printing. The imagery can be realistic, fanciful or completely abstract. Donna Read hand-paints her free, stylized flowers onto velvet cloth using a wide artist's brush (see above left), while Anne-Marie Cadman creates bright designs, based on geometric shapes, squiggles and swirls (see p.131). Bettina Mitchell's cushions are inspired by medieval manuscripts and calligraphy (see p.133). Working on silk, she often uses a warm parchment colour for her background and then silkscreen prints designs in black Procion and acid dyes. Sometimes she applies additional colour by hand afterward.

A plain lampshade takes on a completely new appearance after a coat of fabric paint. You can decorate shades in a variety of different ways – from freehand painting to stencilling. Cressida Bell decorates her unique lampshades with bold leaf designs, which she applies by hand using a Chinese watercolour brush.

Glossary

Acid dye: A type of colourant that permanently stains protein fibres.

Adire: The name given to Nigerian indigo-dyed and resist-patterned cloth.

Aniline: A chemical base yielding many colours.

Batik: A resist method for patterning cloth.

Chint: A Hindu word meaning "coloured" and "variegated".

Chintz: A cotton furnishing fabric which is printed with a floral design in several colours onto a light-coloured background.

Diffusing agent: A chemical that encourages dyes to bond and spread across the surface of silk.

Dilutant: A liquid used to reduce the concentration of a dye.

Direct printing: The process of applying mordant and ink or paint simultaneously.

Discharge printing: The process of bleaching or removing colour from previously dyed cloth.

Disperse dyes: Colours that are insoluble in water, but which are applied to fibre by mixing with a dispersing agent.

Dispersing agent: A substance used to keep dye particles evenly distributed in the dyebath.

Drape: A fabric's natural ability to hang and fold.

Dyebath: The liquid in which cloth is dyed.

Fibre: A natural or synthetic thread that may be spun into a yarn.

Filament: A single strand of fibre.

Finishing: The final processes after textile decoration is complete – for example, washing, pressing or dry-cleaning.

Fixative: A treatment used to make dyes or paints permanent.

Fixing: The permanent attachment of paints and dyes to cloth. This process usually involves baking, ironing or pressing the cloth in order to make the colours light- and colour-fast.

Flat-screen printing: A mechanical aid for printing cloth using stationary flat screens arranged in a line.

Frame: A four-sided wooden or metal structure used for stretching cloth prior to painting.

Ground: The foundation surface or background of a cloth.

Gutta percha: A rubberlike substance used in the silk-painting process.

Intaglio: A pattern that is carved or cut into the surface of a material so as to form a hollow.

Lightbox: An illuminated box used for viewing transparencies.

Mordant: A fixing agent employed during or prior to dyeing.

Multi-printing: The technique of printing using more than one screen.

Palampores: Hand-painted cotton from India, frequently decorated with a "Tree of Life" design.

Photosensitive emulsion: A light-sensitive varnish used to mask off areas of a silkscreen.

Pigment: A substance used to add colour to paint or dye.

Plangi: Also known as tie-dye.

Potassium permanganate: A mineral salt used in the dyeing process in order to create different shades of purple.

Print: A repeat pattern, produced by stencilling or silkscreen printing.

Print paste: The consistency in which colour is applied to cloth during textile printing. A print paste typically comprises: dissolved dyes, solvents, thickening agents and mordants.

Print table: A flat, padded worksurface used as a base during screen printing. You can make a print table in the home by covering a kitchen table with an old blanket and a protective waterproof sheet.

Protein fibres: Fibres that originate from living organisms – for example, wool and silk.

Registration: The correct fitting together of all elements and colours of a printed pattern.

Repeat: The exact reproduction of any unit of a design when placed in an exact geometric relationship to it.

Resist: A substance used to preserve the background colour of a cloth during dyeing – for example, wax or rice paste.

Screen engraving: The production of the open and unfilled pattern areas of a screen. The traditional term is still used, although engraving is no longer carried out.

Screen printing: A form of stencil printing through an open mesh, areas of which have been masked off in order to create a pattern.

Solvent: A solution that is capable of dissolving another substance.

Squeegee: The device used to press print paste through the mesh of a screen.

Stannous chloride: A metal salt used for coagulation when mixing dye paste.

Substantive dye: A dye that has a natural affinity with the fibre, and therefore doesn't need to be mixed with a mordant prior to dyeing.

Sulphoxylate: A powerful discharging agent.

Thickener or thickening agent: This substance is added to the dye to make it thick enough for painting or printing onto cloth.

Wetting agent: This substance is added to the wetting bath in preparation for dyeing, in order to reduce the surface tension of the water and to encourage it to penetrate to the capillary spaces of the fibres.

Right: These richly coloured silk lengths were patterned with a linear design using multiple silkscreens. (Jessica Trotman)

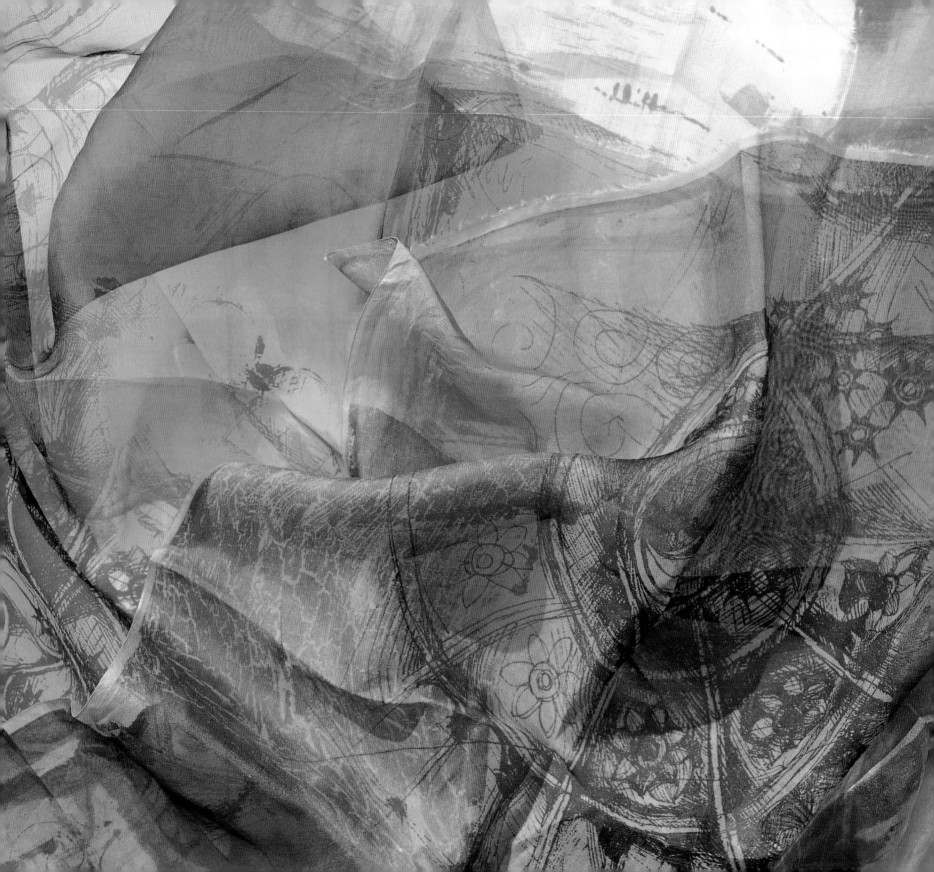

Directory

Ruth Pringle
Sudeley Castle Craft Centre
Winchcombe
Glos GL54 5JD

Carolyn Quartermaine
72 Philbeach Gardens
London SW7

Donna Read
38 Manor Lane
Lewisham
London SE13 5QP

Victoria Richards
Clockwork Studios
38 Southwell Road
London SE5 9PG

Vanessa Robertson
Apple Barn
Week, Dartington
Totnes
Devon TQ9 6JP

Kerry Shaw
3 Bankside
Shelley, Huddersfield
W Yorks HD8 8JD

Pete Shaw
43 Druridge Drive
Newsham Farm Estate
Blyth
Northum NE24 4QY

Ann Smith
4 Downview Rd, Barnham
W Sussex PO22 0EE

Karen Smith
29 Fernhurst Road
Addiscombe, Croydon
Surrey CR0 7DJ

Anna Steiner
2 Kiln Lane
Litchborough, Towcester
Northants NN12 8JQ

Tessuti
Albion Business Centre
78 Albion Road
Edinburgh EH7 5QZ

Timney Fowler
388 Kings Road
London SW3 5UZ

Jessica Trotman
3 Simms Terrace
Gunnislake
Cornwall PL18 9DQ

Michael Walker
40 Ashburnham Grove
London SE10

N. Wickramasinghe
5 Hillcroft Road
Leicester LE5 5DX

Sophie Williams
91 Lausanne Road
London SE15 2HY

Natalie Woolf
10 Wharfedale Street
Leeds LS7 2LF

RECOMMENDED SUPPLIERS

Candle Makers Suppliers
28 Blythe Road
London W14 0HA
Textile supplies and steaming service

Cut Outs
87 Church Road
London W7 3BH
Plain silk and cotton ties

Dylon International
Worsley Bridge Road
London SE26 5HD
Fabric paints and pens

Funn Stockings
PO Box 102
60 High Street
Steyning
W Sussex BN44 3DY
Cotton, silk and wool stockings

Hayes
55 Glengall Road
London SE15 6NF
Paints, dyes and chemicals

Henkel Chemicals
Nopco House
Kirstall Road
Leeds LS3 1JR
Technical information for the textile trade

Inscribe Ltd
Woolmer Industrial Estate
Bordon
Hants GU35 9QE
Fabric paints

John Lewis Partnership
278-306 Oxford Street
London W1
Furnishing fabrics, dress fabrics, fabric paints

Philip and Tacey
North Way
Andover
Hants SP10 5BA
Marbling and silk-painting kits, and fabric supplies

Pongees Ltd
184-186 Old Street
London EC1V 9BP
Silk merchants

Vycombe Ltd
High House
Parnham
Suffolk
Fabric paints

George Weil
18 Hanson Street
London W1P 7DB
Painting and printing supplies (shop and mail order)

COURSES

Camberwell College of Arts
The Decorative Art Department
Peckham Road
London SE5 8UF

Indigo
Whitestone Farmhouse
East Cornworthy
Totnes
Devon TQ9 7HF
Indigo-dyeing and resist-patterning workshops

Manchester Metropolitan University
Faculty of Art and Design
Grosvenor Building
Cavendish Street
Manchester M15 6BR

Vanessa Robertson
Apple Barn
Week
Dartington
Totnes
Devon TQ9 6JP
Tie-dye, wax-resist and vat-dyeing workshops

OTHER USEFUL ADDRESSES

The Batik Guild
3 Vicarage Hill
Badby near Daventry
Northants NN11 6AP

Crafts Council
44a Pentonville Road
Islington
London N1 9BY

Joss Graham
10 Eccleston Street
London SW1W 9LT

Liberty & Company Ltd
210 Regent Street
London W1R 6AH

Arthur Sanderson Ltd
112 Brompton Road
London SW6 1JJ

Warner Fabrics Ltd
Chelsea Garden Market
Chelsea Harbour
Lots Road
London SW10 0XE

$\mathcal{I}ndex$

Acknowledgments

The author and publishers would like to thank all the artists and designers who contributed their work for the book. A special thank you to the following for lending material for the Perspectives and Design Sources chapters: Joss Graham, Warner Fabrics, Arthur Sanderson and Sons Ltd, Timney Fowler Ltd and Liberty of London Prints; and George Weil for lending materials and equipment for the Contents page. Also thanks to Mick Elliot and Graham Smith at Camberwell College of Arts; and Bronwen Hargreaves at the Manchester Metropolitan University.

Mitchell Beazley would like to thank Judy Walker for proof-reading and compiling the index.

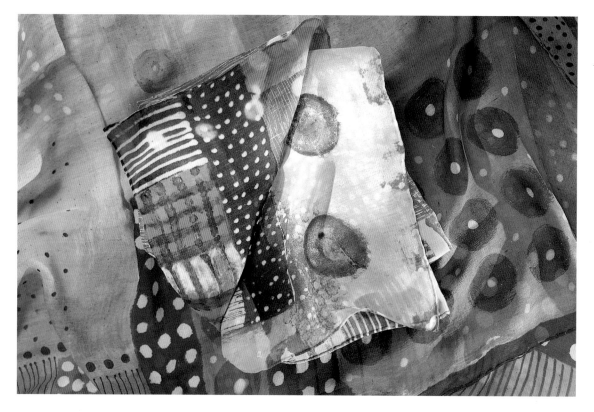

Left: A collection of hand-painted and printed silk scarves. (Sophie Williams)